# CLOSETS

# CLOSETS

## Designing and Organizing the Personalized Closet

Patricia Coen and Bryan Milford

Grove Weidenfeld
New York

**A FRIEDMAN GROUP BOOK**

Published by Grove Weidenfeld
A Division of Wheatland Corporation
841 Broadway
New York, New York 10003-4793

**Library of Congress Cataloging-in-Publication Data**

Coen, Patricia.
Closets: designing and organizing the personalized closet.

1. Storage in the home. 2. Clothes closets.
I. Milford, Bryan. II. Title.
TX309.C64   1987      643'.5   87-8252
ISBN 1-55584-096-5
ISBN 0-8021-3228-6 (pbk.)

*Closets: Designing and Organizing the Personalized Closet*
was prepared and produced by
Michael Friedman Publishing Group, Inc.
15 West 26th Street
New York, New York 10010

Art Director: Mary Moriarty
Designer: Liz Trovato
Photo Editor: Philip Hawthorne
Production: Karen L. Greenberg

Typeset by I, CLAVDIA INC.
Color separations by South Seas Graphic Arts Company Ltd.
Quality Printing and Binding by:
Leefung Asco Printers Ltd.
Yang Industrial Building
830 Lai Chi Kok Road
Kowloon, Hong Kong

First Edition 1988
First Evergreen Edition 1990

10 9 8 7 6 5 4 3

## DEDICATION

For Juanita and William Coen
and Terry and Brian Acworth

## ACKNOWLEDGMENTS

A great many people volunteered their time and expertise during the creation of this book, and we are grateful to all of them. Special thanks go to Joan Halperin, Peter Moore, Maxine Ordesky, Peter Pennoyer, Karen Kaufman-Orloff, Judith Miley, Maynard Hale Lyndon, Lu Lyndon, Linda London, and David Hochberg of the Lillian Vernon Corporation.

# Contents

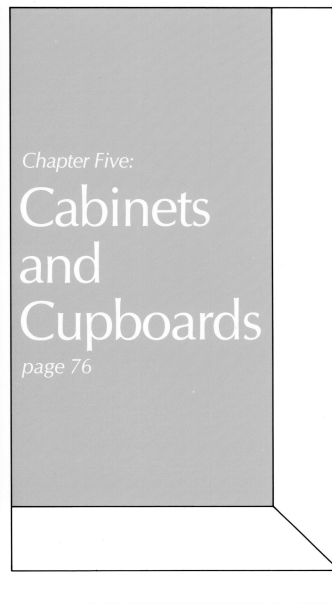

# Chapter One:
# THE DESIGNER'S VIEW

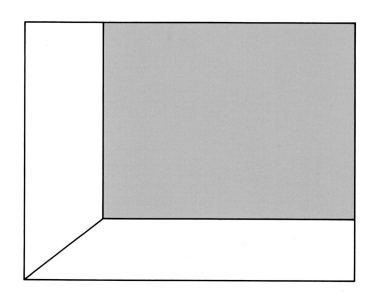

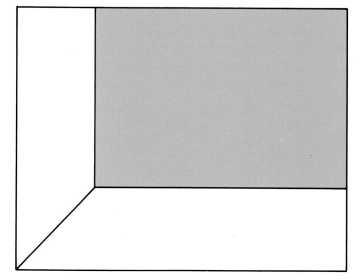

Most people regard their closets—or lack of closets—as a problem. Whether your home is large or small, chances are you do not feel you have enough space to store your clothes and other possessions neatly, attractively, and accessibly. Or, you think you have enough space, but the systems of shelves and rods within that space do not let you organize your possessions as you would like.

Today, you can finally solve both of these problems. In recent years, designers, architects, builders, and manufacturers have turned their attention to solving the complex problem of storage space. Their functional solutions are frequently surprising, often elegant, and always adaptable to almost any home or budget.

# The Root of the Problem

The root of the storage problem is the accumulation of things, or what comedian George Carlin calls "stuff." He developed a classic (and all too accurate) routine that details how people move their "stuff" with them from location to location; the heart of his monologue is the nearly universal truth that no matter how much "stuff" a person tries to discard, there is always too much left to store efficiently. The routine is very funny—until you realize that you are the person he is describing, who cannot jam one more thing into the closet, cabinet, or cupboard. Most people are not smiling as they search in vain for a particular item. Your favorite jacket or skirt or socks, the necktie that makes you look sincere, the linen tablecloth that is spread out only on holidays—these are all potential victims of disorganized clutter. Even if you are lucky and manage to unearth the object of your search, it is likely to be wrinkled, dusty, or in some other way unusable. But there is a solution, and it is all in the approach you take to your closets.

Phillip Ennis/ Design: George Constantin

**Above: This closet illustrates the golden rule of successful closet organization: "a place for everything, and everything in its place." Note that clothing is grouped according to type and dimensions: Folded items are neatly stacked on shelves; shoes are arranged on racks; jackets are grouped together; and so on. You can adapt the principles used in this luxurious closet to your own.**

**Right: A professionally designed closet does more than store clothing—it showcases it. This closet and its contents are as attractive and carefully planned as any other room in the house. While you may not be interested in anything quite this spectacular, the design elements here—especially the lighting—are worth considering in most homes.**

# The Modern Approach to Storage

Today's designers have to meet many more demands when dealing with storage space than they did as little as ten years ago. In the past, people accumulated possessions until the space they lived in became full. Then, instead of throwing unnecessary items away, the average person searched for a new, and bigger, living space. Apartment dwellers moved to houses, and homeowners looked for bigger houses.

In recent years, however, economic realities and the scarcity of available living space have eroded these habits. People are staying in the homes they have and adapting them to their changing needs. They are expecting the most from the money they spend, and are, therefore, taking better care of the goods they buy and keeping them for longer. This represents not only an enormous shift in consumers' attitudes; it also represents a tremendous potential for designers and manufacturers of closets, storage spaces, and storage accessories. As Neil Balter, founder and president of California Closets, Inc., puts it, "the business of closet design and planning has grown because in economic bad times people *need* organization to make things last; in economic good times, they *want* it."

A great deal of today's leader-

ship in design is a natural evolution of the European tradition, in which the "toss it out, buy another one" philosophy never prevailed. For centuries, Europeans have been acutely aware of the importance of using their resources—including money and possessions—as wisely and as conservatively as possible, an attitude that is manifested in the small yet highly productive gardens found in residential sections of major European cities. Today, European and American designers are applying these same principles to create storage systems that give the user maximum space and flexibility. This attitude requires designers—and people designing their own storage spaces—to think about the space first, considering how much room they have and how to best use it. You do not simply start piling possessions into a closet—you first need to decide which possessions are essential, which need to be most accessible, and how to make the closet suit your specific needs.

*Storage space can often be found in unexpected places. This elegant, traditional-looking sitting room has a surprising number of drawers and shelves worked into its design.*

© Peter Paige

# THE EVOLUTION OF THE CLOSET

"It was the development of closet design as a speciality," says Neil Balter, "that made it possible for virtually anyone to be organized. Everything has its particular place—people want to be free of confusion and chaos. People have so many things now that they need order. People didn't really have that order before. Of course, they also didn't have as many things to store."

Historically, closets have been viewed as vertical boxes. The traditional closet is set into a wall and enclosed by a door that looks exactly like the door into a room. The space contains a rod for hanging clothes and a shelf above it to store foldable items or to act as a catch-all for things that will not fit anyplace else. This "old-fashioned" closet offers limited options for organization and is rapidly becoming a thing of the past.

Today's designers recognize the importance of versatility and style in storage spaces and so are exploring far more imaginative, less conventional options. They are designing units that suit an individual's living space and personality. That may mean the storage area is suspended from the ceiling, or that it divides the living space at shoulder height.

According to Maynard Hale Lyndon, an accomplished designer and the founder of Placewares, a chain of exceptional shops specializing in places to put things, "Today, the goal is to create new and more functional spaces within existing space, giving a person considerably more value and use for otherwise wasted or underutilized areas." This view of closets means more than just expanding the physical size of the closet "box" by knocking down walls. It involves equipping all levels and aspects of the "box" with a variety of shelves, rods, hangers, bins, and baskets placed at different heights to suit different needs.

**Left: This room divider provides generous storage space while contributing to privacy. A more traditional room divider would simply waste floor space.**

**Right: Compact yet infinitely useful, this unit illustrates the importance of integrating storage space into a room divider.**

Courtesy Home Magazine/ Photo: Jeff McNamara

*Left: This relatively small area derives an abundance of storage space from a carefully planned assortment of cabinets and shelves. Note the shallow shelving which is used to accommodate small, frequently used items.*

*Right: A wall of shelves helps give this office its cool, uncluttered look.*

*Below: This comfortable, modern room uses storage space as an integral part of its design. Possessions are neatly stored, yet visible and easily accessible.*

# THE "HIGH-TECH" (R)EVOLUTION

Many of the new approaches and products that have revolutionized closet design were originally created for industrial use. Businessmen and manufacturers, who know that space costs money,

tended to be much more vocal and rigid about their storage needs than the average consumer. The design industry accommodated their demands, developing innovative systems of baskets and shelves that have recently been adapted for home use. Consider the flat, chrome baskets created for the donut baker's trade eventually found their way into private homes as attractive and space efficient storage trays. Most restaurant shelves had openwork bottoms because a busy restaurateur did

© Peter Paige/ Design: Antine/Polo Ltd.

© Peter Paige/ Design: Arnold Syrop, AIA

not have time to worry about dusting them. The homeowner was not shown the same consideration—dusting shelves at home was, until recently, a given.

Eventually, the storage system industry recognized the value of the high-tech concept—affordable practicality. They modified the products' commercial look, making them more attractive and stylish, therefore suitable for use in any style home. When these industrial products were first placed in homes, they were given the label "high-tech." This term is used less frequently today, but the products are widely accepted as innovative and efficient works of design.

A natural outgrowth of "high-tech" is wire shelf and basket systems. The wire shelving business is one of the largest and most successful industries created by this minor storage revolution. "Once the wire shelves and storage baskets common in commercial areas were offered to individuals for home use," says Maynard Hale Lyndon, "most people wondered how they managed without them. These wire products are easy to install and easy to cut to size. They have a tremendous application to the home and as a result a whole growth industry has been fostered." Now there are clear boxes, frames, baskets in a variety of colors and finishes, slings, and brackets—a nearly endless variety of items that create efficient storage space out of practically nothing.

If you are planning a do-it-yourself closet reorganization, without the aid of a designer or of customized installation systems, take some time to learn about the variety of shelves, boxes, baskets, and grids that are available and the options they offer; many are illustrated in the pages that follow.

# Help From the Professionals

If your budget permits you to seek the advice of a designer for your storage spaces, he or she will recommend the storage accessory options that are best for your situation. However, even if you are planning to go that route, it is a good idea to become familiar with the products that are available before consulting your designer. That way you can discuss your needs more specifically. "It is important that a client be able to define what the problem is," says George Roach, a designer and the founder of Closetworks. "No one can create a solution without first discussing the problem with the person who lives with it."

"Professionals design a closet to fit your needs," notes Joyce Turner, president of The Closet Doctor. "What is needed is a more personalized, customized design than most people have been used to."

A professionally designed closet can be a wonderful combination of practicality and luxury. The recommendations of a professional designer may change your mundane closet into an innovative storage system that makes your home more attractive and your life easier.

*Above: Not all closets should look like closets. This elegant wooden door conceals a storage area.*

*Right: This well-planned closet illustrates several innovative ways to deal with accessories and awkwardly shaped items.*

Jessica Strang/ Design: Lou Klein

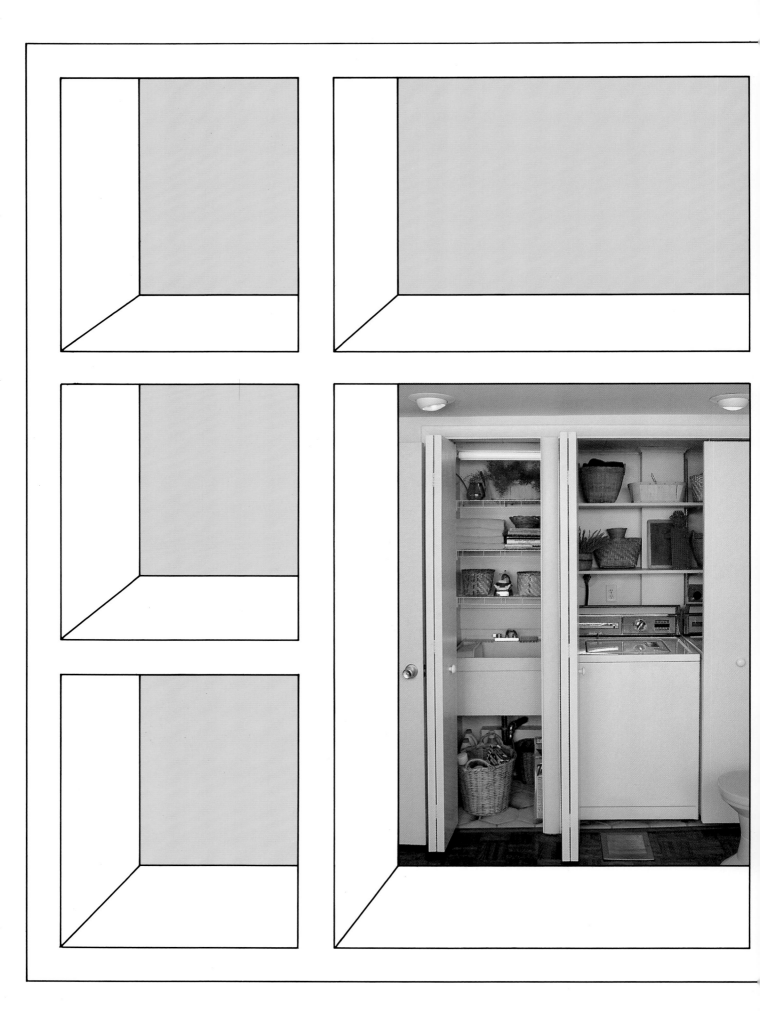

# Chapter Two:
# CHECKPOINTS

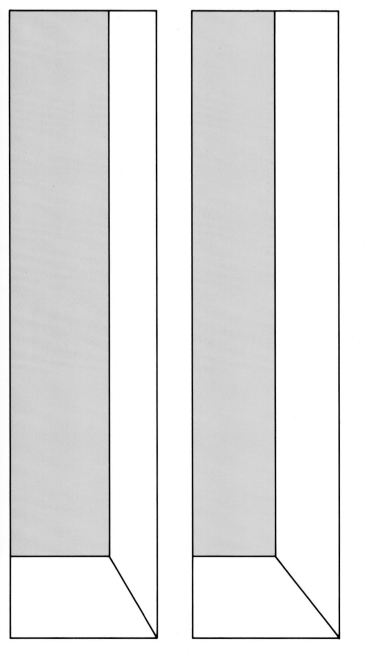

Before approaching a designer and asking him or her to redo your closets, or before choosing a pre-fabricated storage system or assembling a collection of shelves, baskets, hooks, and hangers yourself, give some serious thought to your closet needs. Do not rush this thinking process—it is the most important part of creating a new closet system. Remember, you will have to live with your new system (including mistakes caused by haste) for a long time.

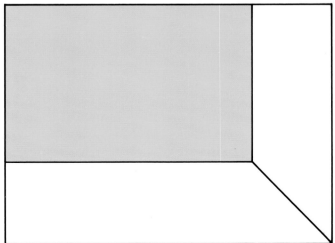

# Figuring Your Needs

There is no magic formula for creating the perfect closet. Instead, the seven steps below will help you define "perfection" for yourself. Follow these steps for each storage space in your home before making any final decisions. You will be surprised at how your plans may change when you see all the options available.

## THE CHECKLIST

1. Throw out excess, unused items.
2. Measure the space(s).
3. Plan for easy retrieval.
4. Evaluate your needs.
5. Add up the space you need.
6. Sort out the details.
7. Draw a diagram.

## Step 1: Throw Out Excess, Unused Items.

This is probably the most important—and toughest—part of reorganizing your storage spaces. One of the biggest causes of clutter is the fact that we frequently add new possessions to our closets without removing old, unused items. The ideal (if somewhat unrealistic) plan is to throw away one item every single time you bring a new one into the house. However, this step requires you to be even more ruthless. Now you must permanently eliminate all items that simply are not worth the storage space. Do not throw away only enough to squeeze in the new possessions. For your reorganization to be effective, throw away every impractical and unused item, leaving empty space.

## Consider your goals

You might assume that the ultimate goal of redoing and organizing your closets is to find enough space to hold all of your current possessions neatly and accessibly. In reality, that is only part of it. A truly successful closet reorganization is one that lets you store all of your current possessions neatly *and* leaves you some empty space to accommodate new acquisitions in the future. Do not be intimidated by a bit of empty space—just let it sit there until you need it.

*Above: A pegboard, hooks, and baskets will help you get the most out of any closet. Note the total absence of wasted space—this closet is useful right up to the ceiling.*

*Facing page: This general-purpose closet uses shelves of different heights and widths to maximize efficiency. Without the shelving, an array of items would dominate the space.*

"At least once a year, I spend a weekend throwing things out," says designer Joan Halperin. "I spent one New Year's Day cleaning my closets, and I must have filled the incinerator chest-high at least six times. The last time I cleaned out my closets, I looked critically at them—they are fairly basic New York City apartment closets, with one hanging rod and two shelves above—and I noticed that I could easily add a third shelf above the other two, increasing the shelf space by a third, which is quite a lot.

"I have found that many people call me for advice," she continues, "and when I look at their closets I see that they are really very well planned and there are no problems in terms of adequate hanging rods or shelving. The problem comes from the fact that the people have never straightened the closets up or thrown anything away. Sometimes, the solution is as simple as that."

In order to properly clean out your closets, begin with a realistic attitude and a firm resolve to succeed. Look at each item and ask yourself, "Do I really like this? Do I really use it? Do I really need it? Do I really have room for it?" If you find that you have more negative than positive answers, you should think twice about putting that item in your "to keep" pile. Make the task less stressful by cultivating a practical and positive attitude. For example, that bulky sweater that looks terrible on you

may seem difficult to throw away because it was a gift from a favorite relative. But look at it this way—by keeping the unflattering sweater, you are wasting storage space that could better be used for other things, and wasting energy by having to dig past it every time you want something in the closet.

When putting things away for seasonal storage, note which items you really used during the season just past, and which ones you did not. Perhaps some of these unused items can be updated and made more appealing with some alterations; anything that cannot be altered or is worse for wear should be thrown away.

This process of discarding items may seem to take a long time, but it will be most successful if you do not force yourself to do it quickly. Plan to spend at least an hour a week eliminating the excess. Whenever possible, donate useable items to charity. You will feel better about your loss, and the recipients will appreciate your thoughtfulness.

Do not be discouraged as you work on discarding your clutter. Be aware that there will be times when you feel like you have created a bigger mess than you can ever clean up; instead of clutter unobtrusively stashed behind closet doors, it is now out in the open, in piles mentally labeled "to keep," "to throw away," "for charity," and "I'm not sure yet." Do not give up—you will get through it, and you will be glad you did.

## Step 2: Measure the Space(s).

Paring down your possessions is only the beginning—now you have to figure out how to best use the storage space available for them. Carefully consider whether this particular closet is the best place for each item you plan to put back. You may find that items you have always stashed in your bedroom would go better in the front hall closet. Now, while everything is out of the closet, is a good time to analyze just what belongs where.

Measure and record the dimensions of each closet in your home, including width, depth, and clearance space for existing shelves and door closure. Do not forget to consider the back of the door and wall surfaces as potential storage areas. The measurements should help you decide what would be ideally stored in each closet.

**Right: An elegant, lighted walk-in closet can double as a dressing room. Here, rarely used and out-of-season clothing is stacked on the higher shelves: More frequently used items are placed within easy reach.**

## Step 3: Plan for Easy Retrieval.

The most important thing about storage space is *not* where to put things away—it is the ease with which you can take them out again. "Retrieval is the key to storage," says Joan Halperin. "You can store things in boxes in the cellar, but that is not what people want to do because that makes it too hard to get things out when you need them. Plan to store things where you actually use them. Sit down and ask yourself, 'how often do I really need to take this vacuum cleaner out…how often do I do the laundry…where can I put this to save some steps…where do I re-

ally need to keep the typing paper.' This will help you to think about a space, and how you move within that space. If you end up storing something you need frequently in a place that is nearly inaccessible, then you might as well not have it at all."

Ideally, every item should be stored as near to where it will be used as possible. Sporting goods should be near an outside door rather than buried in an upstairs clothes closet; clothing should be in or near the bedroom, dressing room, or bathroom; outerwear should be near the front door.

*Jessica Strang*

**Above: This photo and the one at right illustrate two different approaches to the same space. Here, the storage unit is closed, forming an unobtrusive wall. Note that even normally wasted overhead space is utilized.**

**Right: The same storage unit is shown without shades, so that the shelving and its contents become part of the room's design. This approach lends a more open, casual look to the room.**

## Step 4: Evaluate Your Needs.

Once you have decided on the general use of a particular closet, take stock of everything you have to store in that space (i.e. shoes, clothing, linens, sporting goods, and so on). Write it all down. Now, look again. What do you really *have* to store in this space? Keep in mind that most clothes are seasonal, so maybe out-of-season items can be moved to another area. Storing out-of-season clothes in an organized, space-saving way allows more room for the clothes you are currently using. You are also saved from having to look through extra out-of-season items to find what you want for the day.

Next, make a list detailing the ideal contents of every closet in your house. The reality of your situation may demand that you compromise a bit when you actually put things away, but the list will have helped you determine your priorities.

Jessica Strang

## The standard measurements

Your particular needs will, of course, dictate your closet plan, but there are some architectural standards you can use as a guideline.

The primary function of a closet dictates its ideal depth:

—linens and household equipment need a space at least 20 inches (54 cm) deep.

—clothes closets should measure from 24 to 32 inches (61 to 81 cm) deep (although many closets in newer apartments and condo townhouses measure closer to 22 inches (56 cm).

—when using wire shelving or shoe racks, allow 12 inches (30 cm) minimum between shelves for bracketing purposes. When spacing shelves, take into account exactly what it is you want to store and allow enough clearance room for those items.

—for double-hung clothes (jackets, shirts, skirts, and pants hung one above the other), the hanging rods should be about 42 and 82 inches (107 and 208 cm) from the floor.

—determine the vertical space necessary for your particular clothing needs by measuring your longest garment plus the hanger neck, and adding 4 inches (10 cm) to the total.

## A sample list

Here is one woman's idea of the perfect bedroom closet. What would your list include? Remember, it is not enough to simply fit all of these things in a closet with no room to spare. There should be at least 2 inches (5 cm) of space between each item to allow air to circulate freely to prevent mustiness and wrinkling.

**Room for a dozen dresses**

**Space for 25 pairs of shoes**

**Storage for accessories (handbags, scarves, belts)**

**A place to hang necklaces**

**Space to stack folded items, eliminating a dresser**

**A laundry hamper**

### Adult's Closet

This list offers the average dimensions of the most commonly worn articles of men and women's clothing. These obviously need not all be kept in the same closet.

Man's coat: 50 inches (127 cm) long; 22 inches (56 cm) wide.

Woman's coat: 52 inches (132 cm) long; 16 inches (41 cm) wide.

Woman's dress: 48 inches (122 cm) long; 13 inches (33 cm) wide.

Man's suit jacket: 38 inches (97 cm) long; 20 inches (51 cm) wide.

Woman's skirt: 35 inches (89 cm) long; 13 inches (33 cm) wide.

Folded sweater: 14 inches (36 cm) deep; 10 inches (25 cm) wide.

Folded shirt: 14 inches (36 cm) deep; 8 inches (20 cm) wide.

Man's shoes: 12 inches (30 cm) long; 9 inches (23 cm) wide.

Woman's shoes: 10 inches (25 cm) long; 7 inches (18 cm) wide.

Handbag: 3 inches (8 cm) deep; 11 inches (28 cm) wide.

Man's hat: 6 inches (15 cm) deep; 11 inches (28 cm) wide.

Courtesy Clairson International

**Child's Closet**
These dimensions reflect the needs of a child who is about ten years old; you will have to adjust them according to your child's age and size.
Pants: 20 inches (51 cm) long; 9 inches (23 cm) deep.

Folded sweater: 11 inches (28 cm) deep; 9 inches (23 cm) wide.

Folded shirt: 11 inches (28 cm) deep; 8 inches (20 cm) wide.

Jacket: 24 inches (61 cm) long; 12 inches (30 cm) wide.

Shoes: 8 inches (20 cm) long; 9 inches (23 cm) wide.

Folded pajamas: 11 inches (28 cm) deep; 8 inches (20 cm) wide.

## Step 5: Add Up the Space You Need.

To determine the amount of space you need, group items as you plan to store them. For a clothes closet, gather together accessories, dress clothes, sports clothes, evening gowns, nightclothes, shoes, and, if you do not have a separate closet for it, outerwear. In the kitchen, sort serving trays, appliances, glassware, cutlery, and so on. Consider each category as a whole so you can evaluate the type and the amount of storage space needed for each group.

After you have decided which items belong in each closet, take careful note of the general dimensions of each item to give you an idea of how much space they require. Some essential items frequently stored in closets—sports equipment, a laundry hamper, a small stepladder—take up large amounts of space, as do other awkwardly shaped items. You may decide their storage is easiest to handle by putting them together in a closet of their own, perhaps in a hallway or near the kitchen. For items that require a storage accessory, such as a box or a basket, be sure to measure each item and the accessory together.

To save you the time and trouble of measuring every item of clothing, here is a list of the general dimensions of most kinds of clothing and commonly sorted household items. This list will help you figure out the rough dimensions of your ideal closet(s). You may choose to arrange the possessions in your closets differently than shown in our list, depending upon your needs and number of closets.

### Linen Closet

Blanket: 12 inches (30 cm) deep; 16 inches (41 cm) wide; 4 inches (10 cm) high.

Sheets: 14 inches (36 cm) deep; 10 inches (25 cm) wide; 1 inch (3 cm) high.

Pillowcases: 11 inches (28 cm) deep; 7 inches (18 cm) wide; ¾ inch (2 cm) high.

Bath towels: 13 inches (33 cm) deep; 13 inches (33 cm) wide; 2 inches (6 cm) high.

Washcloths: 9 inches (23 cm) deep; 4 inches (10 cm) wide; ½ inch (1 cm) high.

USA Kartell

### Cleaning/Sundries Closet

If you have the luxury of a separate closet for cleaning equipment and supplies and/or items of awkward shapes, consider installing shelves on only one side of it. The shelves can hold bottles, brushes, sponges, buckets, and other items of similar size; tall items can stand in the unshelved side.

Vacuum cleaner: 43 inches (109 cm) tall; 10 inches (25 cm) wide at its base.

Broom: 58 inches (147 cm) tall; 8 inches (20 cm) wide at its base.

Dustpan: 8 inches (20 cm) deep; 10 inches (25 cm) wide.

Brush: 12 inches (30 cm) long.

Bucket: 12 inches (30 cm) tall; 10 inches (25 cm) wide.

James R. Levin

### Hall Closet

Here, a hall closet is any in which you choose to store awkwardly shaped items, or any items that do not fit into your clothes and linen closets. Accessories and sports equipment are the two categories most commonly found in the hall closet.

Umbrella: 36 inches (91 cm) tall.

Briefcase: 5 inches (13 cm) deep; 21 inches (53 cm) wide; 12 inches (30 cm) tall.

Camera bag: 7 inches (18 cm) deep; 13 inches (33 cm) wide; 9 inches (23 cm) tall.

Tennis racket: 9 inches (23 cm) wide; 36 inches (91 cm) tall.

Baseball mitt: 10 inches (25 cm) wide.

Ball: 9 inches (23 cm) wide.

## Step 6: Sort out the details.

Once you have chosen the best location for your possessions, you must decide how to place them within the space. Consider your personal preferences and habits. For example, would you be comfortable placing your shoes up on a high shelf or hanging them in shoe bags? Or would you be happiest kicking them off onto a low shelf rack? If you are not comfortable with the arrangement of your closet, you probably will not bother putting things back in their proper places.

Look at each category of items to be stored. Note how accessible each must be, then consider the options. Clothes may be hung on hangers, hooks, or racks, or they can be folded on shelves, in open wire baskets or closed boxes. New York architect and designer Peter Moore suggests you consider alternatives to hangers. "Gravity doesn't do anything for most clothes," he says.

"I think anything you can lay flat should be laid flat. Hang things that are easiest to hang, such as coats and jackets, but it is a good idea to put shirts and even trousers on shelves or trays if you can." Corner shelves, basket storage, open wire shelving, open wire drawers, or trays are only a few of the options available.

Shoes can be hung in a shoe bag on the back of the door, lined up on a shelf off the floor, or hung in a shoe stack from the closet rod. Long hanging clothes should be grouped together in one area. Short hanging clothes can be double-hung. There may be room for shelves and/or basket storage for folded clothes inside your closet, either above or below short hanging clothes.

Whenever possible, keep as many items as possible off the floor. Floor storage almost automatically equals uncontrollable clutter; there simply is not room for a lot of stuff on the floor of any closet, no matter how spacious or well designed that closet may be.

Remember, the measurements you took in Step 5 are important,

but they are not the only thing to consider. While ironing out the details keep in mind the size of the person(s) using the closet. Do not plan to install a shelf that is higher than you can comfortably reach unless you are going to use it to store out-of-season or infrequently used items. Also, if you decide you would like to use baskets in your closet, make sure there is plenty of room for them to slide in and out.

Give some thought to the most attractive and appropriate doors for your closets. The basic types—sliding, folding, and hinged—each have advantages and disadvantages. The primary disadvantage of sliding or folding doors is the fact that you cannot use the inside of

the doors for additional storage. The interior of a hinged door on a deep closet can be used for hanging shoe hooks, racks, or bags; belts; or tie racks and hooks. Folding doors and hinged doors offer easy access to the entire closet, while overlapping sliding doors let you view only half at a time.

Peter Pennoyer, designer and architect, says "The items in your closets should be able to breathe a bit." Cramming items together, even if they are arranged neatly, will cause wrinkles and mustiness. You can avoid stuffiness by outfitting your closets with louvered doors, or you can bore tiny, barely perceptible holes through solid doors to keep air circulating.

*Right: A media center is cleverly and elegantly built into a master bedroom. English-style storage cabinet contains shelves of different heights and widths. Concealed within are a television set, stereo unit, and other electronic equipment.*

## Step 7: Draw a diagram.

Once you have selected the type of storage that will best suit your needs, double-check the dimensions you took earlier to make sure items fit where you have planned them. Take a piece of graph paper or tissue paper and map out your closet plan. Sketch into it all the items you plan to store so you will have an overall idea of how the

closet will look. A good scale to use is each half inch (1.25 cm) equals one foot (30cm).

Now here is a special reward for all your hard work. You may find that you have saved so much space reorganizing your existing closets that you have ended up with an empty one. If it is big enough, consider using it as a tiny

extra room. With the addition of the appropriate shelving, small desk, or other equipment, you can turn a closet into a work area, sewing room, or home office. If it is too small for alternative uses, decide now what will be stored there in the future and look forward to filling it up in an organized, deliberate fashion.

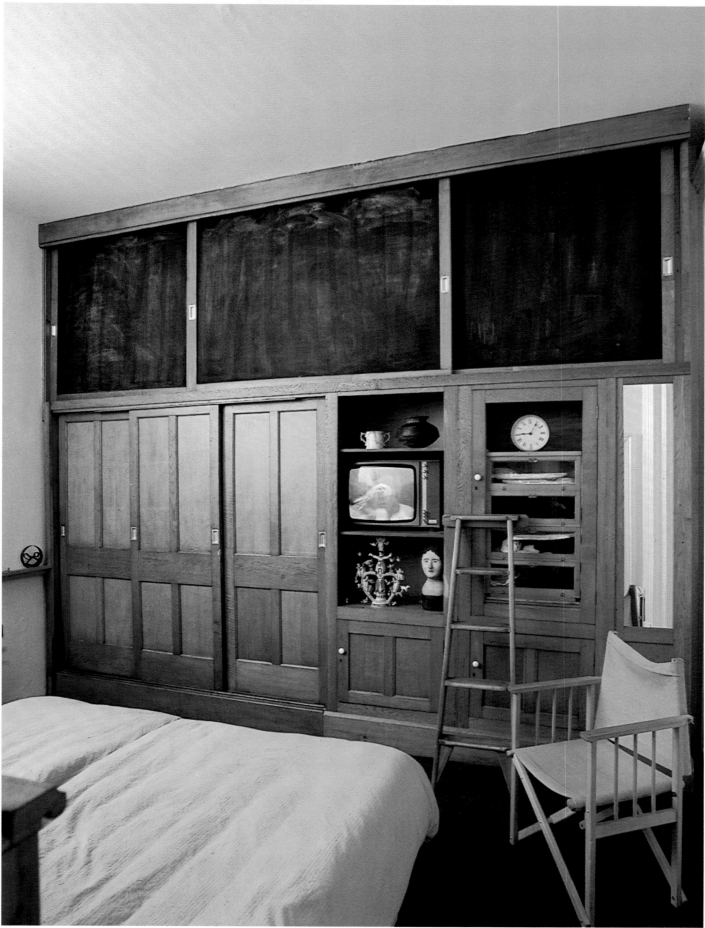

Jessica Strang/ Designer: Bob Gill

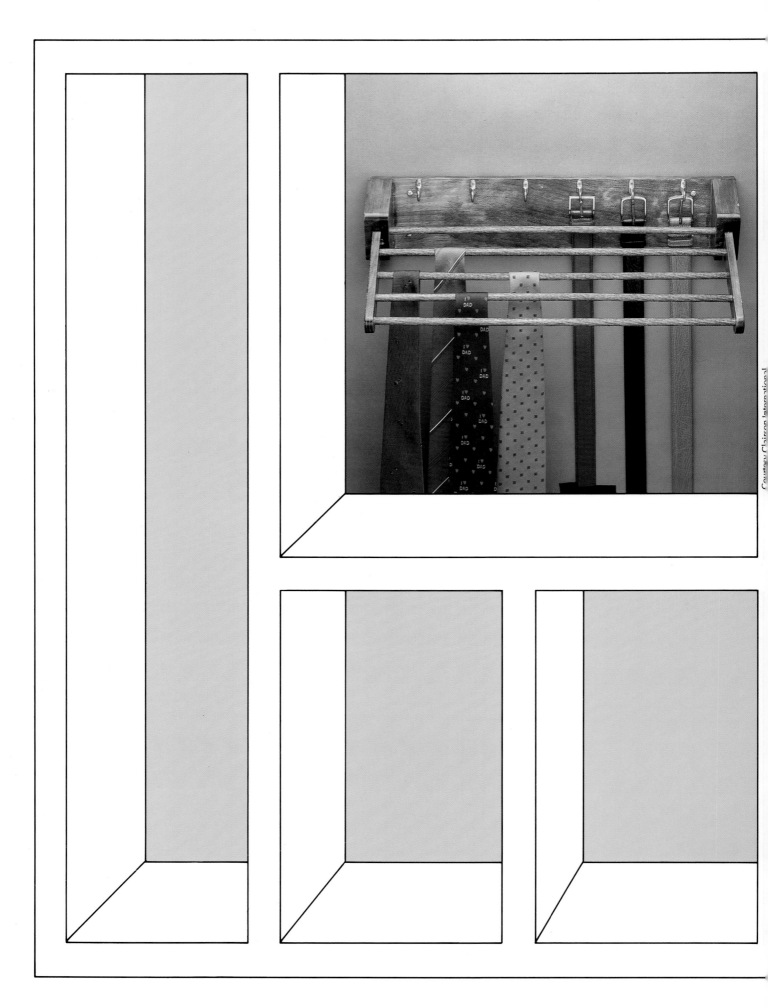

# Chapter Three:
# THE
# ORGANIZERS

As more and more people recognized the fact that moving into a new home to buy more storage space was an impractical luxury, they looked for ways to create more storage space within their present homes. These circumstances provided the ideal environment for the growth of the closet organizer concept, and a myriad of clever install-it-yourself products that are the result of this dramatic change in the attitudes of both manufacturers and consumers.

# Ready-to-Use Systems

Builders and homeowners no longer feel limited by the "traditional" vertical spaces in closets, laundry rooms, bathrooms, and pantries. Their options have been extended by the availability of versatile units such as ventilated shelves, wall and door racks, undershelf accessories, stacking drawers, and other storage accessories that can be combined to create hard-working, easily installed systems that address a wide range of storage problems.

You will get the most out of these ready-to-use systems if you do not limit your thinking by assuming that all closets must look the same, or that every closet must fit into the traditional form. "People can be too timid," says Joan Halperin. "It's best to consider a whole wall [within a closet] vertically and horizontally for storage space. Using the entire area will give you much more storage space. Using the entire area will give you much more storage, and it will look less cluttered." By putting every cubic foot of storage to good use, organizer systems can make your stored items easily accessible, visible, and well ventilated.

*Right: These shelves and baskets transform a raw closet space into an all-purpose storage area without any wasted space.*

*Facing page: The capacity of this relatively small closet was more than doubled by the addition of shelves.*

Courtesy of Poggenpohl

# BASKETS AND SHELVES

Because fabric must be able to breathe to keep from getting musty, ventilated shelves and baskets are a valuable aid in clothing care. They also minimize the amount of dust that can settle on items within a closet; most of the new systems with epoxy or rubber finishes do not collect dust.

Multipurpose organizers designed to serve several different functions are widely available. Remarkable open wire basket and shelving systems make it possible to store shirts, hats, shoes, sweaters, underwear, lingerie, socks—virtually all wardrobe accessories—in a relatively small area.

One basic multipurpose organizer system from Closet Maid is made up of 12-inch (30-cm) squares hooked together to create an elaborate shelving system. It requires almost no installation because it hangs from a rod.

Companies such as Elfa, Closet Maid, Robolo, and Corr-Pak, to name just a few of the leaders in the industry, have developed systems that include adjustable shelves, rods, and hangers as well as both wall-hung and freestanding brackets and frames that hold baskets for the various categories of clothing. Shelves are adjustable for height and also tilt for special uses such as shoe storage. All you need to put them in place yourself is a screwdriver, a level, and (in some cases) a drill. Thanks to these systems, installing a whole storage system is no more difficult than hanging a bookshelf.

*Open shelving (facing page) is ideal for those sweaters, shirts, and other items one wears every day. Shoe slots beneath are positioned at an ideal height for visibility and reach. No more bending and scrambling around in the dark for that matching loafer or pump.*

## Basket Systems

Freestanding basket-style organizers, intended for both home and office use, let you build a storage space that features particularly easy access to your belongings. A basic unit consists of the frame, which can be of varying height, (for particularly tall storage, you can stack one unit atop another); the crossbars, which determine the width of the unit; and the baskets. The baskets come in different widths to fit the frame and crossbars you choose; all widths are usually available in depths from about 1 to 10 inches (3 to 25 cm). There are also flat shelves that can be inserted into the frames or used on top of the unit, giving you a bit of extra work surface or storage space. The freestanding units can be placed in or outside of a closet, and they can be assembled easily using only a hammer.

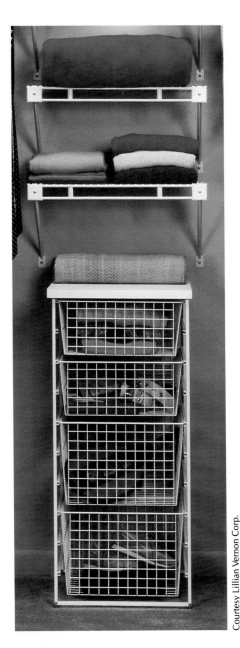

*A wire basket system (left) provides top-to-bottom, easy access to belongings of varying shapes and sizes. Great for sweaters, belts, and odds-and-ends, the baskets keep all kinds of clutter tucked neatly away. The system here also provides a handy tabletop surface.*

Courtesy Lillian Vernon Corp.

*Shelf dividers (below) are particularly helpful when used on a high shelf that is invariably difficult to reach. Open wire dividers like these keep clothes, hats, and accessories well-ventilated, accessible, and easily identifiable.*

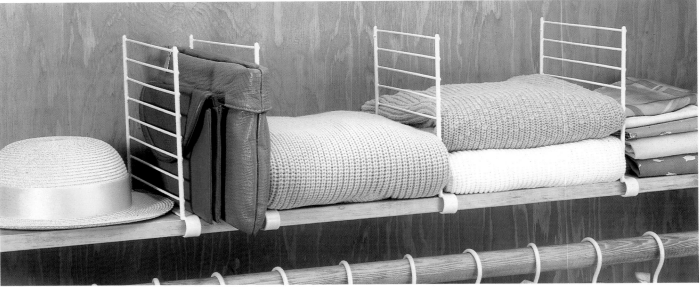

Courtesy Lillian Vernon Corp.

Combine as many units as you need to create a complete personally tailored system. For example, two units of the same height will support a desk-top in a home office (office supplies can be stored in the baskets). Or you may wish to create a "linen closet" in the bathroom—the open baskets are ideal for letting air circulate around your linens in a damp bathroom. Use the units inside a closet to organize space, or store clothes outside of the closet in them. In the kitchen, they will hold canned goods and awkwardly shaped items that don't fit well in cupboards and drawers. Because the units can be tailored to almost any height and width, you can convert previously wasted spaces into storage areas.

## Shelves and Racks

Easy-to-install shelves and racks can turn awkward or unused areas into storage spaces. Slanted racks will hold shoes neatly; shelves placed high in a closet offer ideal storage space for out-of-season items that do not require easy access.

**Below: These special clothing racks let you put several items on one hanger, thus reducing the amount of space needed along the hanging rod.**

# HANGERS

Even with shelves, racks, baskets, and bins in place, the hanging rod remains an important part of most closets. And, although many designers criticize hanging clothes and encourage alternatives, there is really no way to eliminate completely the need for the hanging rod. You can, however, minimize potential damage to your clothes and get the most out of hanging your clothes by choosing the proper hangers.

Never use ordinary wire hangers. They will leave thin ridges in the shoulders of garments, and they may rust, leaving permanent stains on your clothing. When all you need is an ordinary hanger for a suit, shirt, or pants, choose one coated with non-slip vinyl. With these multicolored hangers, think about color coding your clothes, putting separates that complement one another on hangers of the same color.

If you have several pairs of pants to hang, save space with a multiple-rod trouser hanger that lets you drape one pair neatly over another. You will be able to hang three or four pairs of pants in the space required for one. Multiple-clamp skirt hangers are also available.

If your closets are spacious, consider hanging your sheets there. You can get an extra large, heavy-duty hanger that lets you hang sheets and blankets to conserve space in your linen closet.

Courtesy Lillian Vernon Corp.

**Above: These hanger extenders let some items hang below others to increase the capacity of the hanging rod and keep clothes from being jammed together so that they don't wrinkle.**

41

Bill Rothschild/Design: Judith Kashden of "Closet Systems"

Courtesy Lillian Vernon Corp.

## HOOKS AND GRIDS

An array of hooks and grids, placed both in closets and outside of them, can serve as attractive and efficient catchalls to keep clothing and miscellaneous items from piling up on the furniture. You can find a color and style to suit virtually every decor. Make sure you consider your specific needs before you buy hooks. A lightweight hook will do for the back of the bathroom door to hold nightwear; a heavier hook is necessary to hang coats by the front door. Some hooks are attached to a surface with adhesive; others have to be inserted into a hole drilled in the door. Make sure you check the installation instructions for a hook before you buy.

Grids, which can have small baskets hooked onto them to expand storage, are an excellent choice to store and organize small items in the kitchen, bathroom, or kids' rooms. Consider hanging cooking utensils from them, using them to hold personal appliances in the bathroom, or hanging school bags and jackets from them.

*Facing page: An assortment of hooks, hangers, baskets, and racks work together to turn an ordinary closet into a spacious and well-organized storage space. These inexpensive products help even an amateur create a closet that is as attractive and efficient as those designed by professionals.*

*Above: Here is a closet in the process of transformation. The addition of these simple accessories—a low hanging rod for trousers and skirts, a shoe rack, and a few shelves—increases the capacity of this closet by at least one-third.*

# BINS

Plastic stackable cubes and bins are an alternative to the basket systems. Most of these modular units, such as the ones made by Robolo, can be equipped with snap-on doors for the front to protect the contents from dust. Like the wire baskets, the bins can be stacked side by side or on top of one another to create a unit that fits almost any space.

Courtesy Lillian Vernon Corp.

*Above: These plastic bins are ideal for storing out-of-season clothing, rarely used items, and sundries that defy categorization. The bins can be stacked on top of one another on the uppermost shelf of a closet. The snap-on lids protect contents from dust.*

*Left: A woven basket serves the same purpose as a bin, but does so much more elegantly. Use baskets to hold small items that tend to be misplaced. Attractive baskets can even be displayed on tabletops and bureaus, where they can act as functional and beautiful temporary storage for guests.*

*Left: This rack can be placed on a closet wall, on the inside of a closet door, or even in plain sight, and used as a catchall for hats, scarves, umbrellas, and other potential sources of clutter.*

Courtesy Lillian Vernon Corp.

*Below: This sliding plastic rack, installed inside a low kitchen cabinet, allows easy access to cleaning products and supplies.*

Courtesy Lillian Vernon Corp.

46

# BAGS

One of the best ways to utilize existing space is to get clothing out of dresser drawers and into hanging garment bags. Consider the possibility of eliminating your dresser entirely—with the proper use of storage systems, you can store all of your clothing in your closets. Many designers agree that a dresser creates more problems than it solves. It does not store things efficiently, and it takes up a lot of valuable floor space that might better hold a chair or more useful piece of furniture. A dresser also renders the floor and air space above it relatively useless—in most cases, the top of a dresser becomes an ugly catchall for clutter.

Today's garment bags are different than the bulky ones you may be familiar with. They are available in a variety of lengths to accommodate different kinds of clothing, and there are even very narrow bags with tiers of canvas "shelves" designed to hold shoes vertically, in a minimum of space. These slim new bags can store shoes that previously would have spread over several square feet of floor space.

Nylon garment bags also help keep out dust and allow clothing to breathe. Air can get in through the nylon, but dust can't. This feature is especially valuable when you realize that dust can slowly wear away at your garments, contributing to their eventual decay.

Any combination of these organizational systems—chosen after you have carefully evaluated your needs—will help you plan your space more efficiently. Used properly, storage accessories and systems can double your closet space.

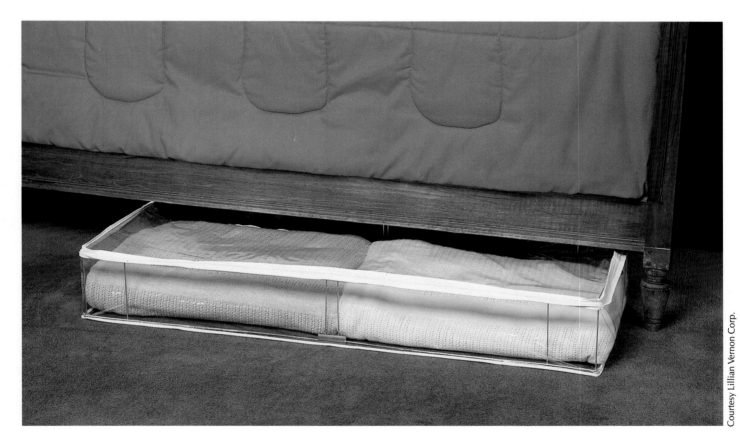

*Courtesy Lillian Vernon Corp.*

***Facing page: This assortment of garment bags maximizes closet capacity while protecting clothing from dust. Note shoes stored in the narrow bag, shirts and sweaters in the shelved bag, and bedding on the floor.***

***Above: Sometimes it is acceptable to keep things under your bed—but only if you can do it as neatly as this. This garment bag allows utilization of an otherwise wasted space.***

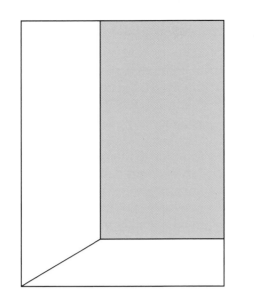
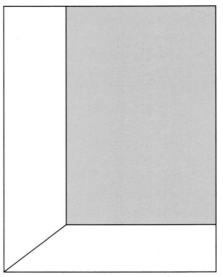
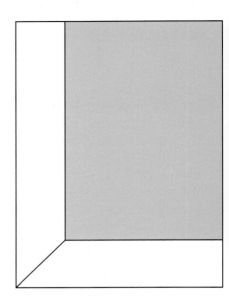

# Chapter Four:
# EXEMPLARY CLOSETS

Although the average person can work wonders reorganizing a closet with the help of commercially available storage systems, some people choose to turn to the experts for help. Professionally designed closets are more costly, but the personalized results can be spectacular.

The pages that follow show and describe closets created by a leading space planner. You may find that some of the innovative techniques used here can be adapted to solve problems in your own home.

# A Custom-Designed Space

Maxine Ordesky, a Beverly Hills-based space designer who specializes in closets, believes that organization is the key to keeping all aspects of life running smoothly. She is the founding president of the National Association of Professional Organizers, a group whose members help clients organize their time, businesses, homes, and lives. Her successful closet remodeling business is a natural outgrowth of her talents as a professional organizer.

"I found that no matter how well I had helped organize a client, if the space was wrong, then the organization didn't work," Ordesky explains. "Then one of my clients asked me to redesign her closets. I told her I wasn't a professional designer, but she asked me to sketch my ideas for a well-organized closet so that she could have a professional construct it. I tried it, and discovered I was good at it. After that, I studied drafting and design and began specializing in closets."

Although Ordesky's closets are undeniably luxurious, their appearance is not her primary consideration. "When I design," she says, "my first and foremost concern is not the way it is going to look, but the way it's going to work. Function and organization come first; the look comes after."

Ordesky's services are costly, but her clients are the first to admit she is well worth the expense. "I charge a consultation and design fee," she says. "And I tell prospec-

*Maxine Ordesky turned her own closet (above) into a walk-in with plenty of room for clothes, shoes and bags. The shoe shelves are close together to conserve vertical space. Cubbies at the top of the shelves keep pocketbooks visible.*

tive clients that if they're viewing the work they want done on their closets in terms of hundreds of dollars, they can't afford me. Some say that they can go to a store that reorganizes closets for far less money. I tell them, 'that's fine, you go talk to them. If they can do exactly what you want, terrific. If they can't, come back and we'll talk again.' Many of them come back."

Ordesky offers far more personalized service and attention, for she designs each closet to suit the most minute details of her clients' lives. One example of Ordesky's attention to detail is the "staging area" she puts in each closet. "The 'staging area' is a partitioned drawer for temporary storage," she explains. "It's where you empty your pockets or purse at the end of the day. It holds change, keys, eyeglasses, wallets—whatever you need to take with you when you leave the house again." She also recommends that clients have a pole for extra hangers installed 2 inches (5 centimeters) below the ceiling of the closet. "Extra hangers shouldn't be taking up space on the hanging bar," she says. The hanger for anything that is being worn should stay in place, and then it will be handy when the clothes are taken off.

Ordesky counts and measures every item that is to fit in each closet, a process that takes at least five or six hours. She talks to the closet's owners and asks them to assess their own needs. "I always ask what the client likes about the present situation," she says. "It's also essential for me to find out what their problems are, what frustrates them. I ask a lot of questions to get that information. I may ask a woman, 'Where do you put your stockngs on? Where do you put your shoes on?' Some of the homes I work in are so large that it's a long walk from the closet to the bed. In those cases, I might put a chair or hassock in the closet so the client can sit down as she dresses."

Ordesky believes that a client's profession and habits influence his

*Here is another view of Ordesky's closet (right). This section is used to hang longer items such as dresses, and coats. The shoes above match the outfits hung on the rod. A belt rack on the wall keeps coordinating belts within easy reach.*

Lois Ellen Frank/Design: Maxine Ordesky, Beverly Hills, California

or her closet needs. A lawyer, for example, needs a lot of space for suits; men who travel a lot need storage space for folded shirts that can be easily tucked into a suitcase. After twelve years of questioning clients, Ordesky has also learned a bit about human nature. "In my experience," she observes, "I have found that men who wear boxer shorts always wear undershirts."

The photographs and blueprints in this chapter detail some of Ordesky's work. Each closet was designed after careful consideration of the client's needs and preferences, and each one is every bit as elegant as the house that surrounds it. However, many of the innovative storage ideas here can be adapted to any space.

Lois Ellen Frank/Design: Maxine Ordesky, Beverly Hills, California

*Here is a view (above) of the closet Ordesky designed for Barney Rosenzweig, producer of the television show* Cagney and Lacy. *The deep shelf above this section of hanging clothes accommodates Rosenzweig's collection of hats.*

*Lois Ellen Frank/Design: Maxine Ordesky, Beverly Hills, California*

*Above: Rosenzweig's closet has shoes conveniently stored on eye level shelves. Underneath the shelves is a countertop, used to hold stacks of folded shirts. The counter serves as a work surface to fold shirts and sweaters.*

*Lois Ellen Frank/Design: Maxine Ordesky, Beverly Hills, California*

*This built-in cabinet unit (left) offers ample storage for sweaters, shirts, socks, scarves, and handkerchiefs. Note that the folded shirts are stacked with collar ends alternating.*

Lois Ellen Frank/Design: Maxine Ordesky, Beverly Hills, California

This woman's closet (left) combines practicality with beautiful design. The closed drawers hold lingerie and nightgowns, the open pull-out shelves hold sweaters and scarves, and the open shelves above hold more sweaters. The countertop can be used as a work surface for folding sweaters and shirts or as a display area for plants, photographs, and favorite objects, giving a personal touch to the closet area.

This tie rack (right) is only 19 inches (48 centimeters) wide, but it can hold 34 ties, each on its own hook. The tie rack is available in most stores that carry closet organizing supplies.

# A Woman's Walk-In Closet

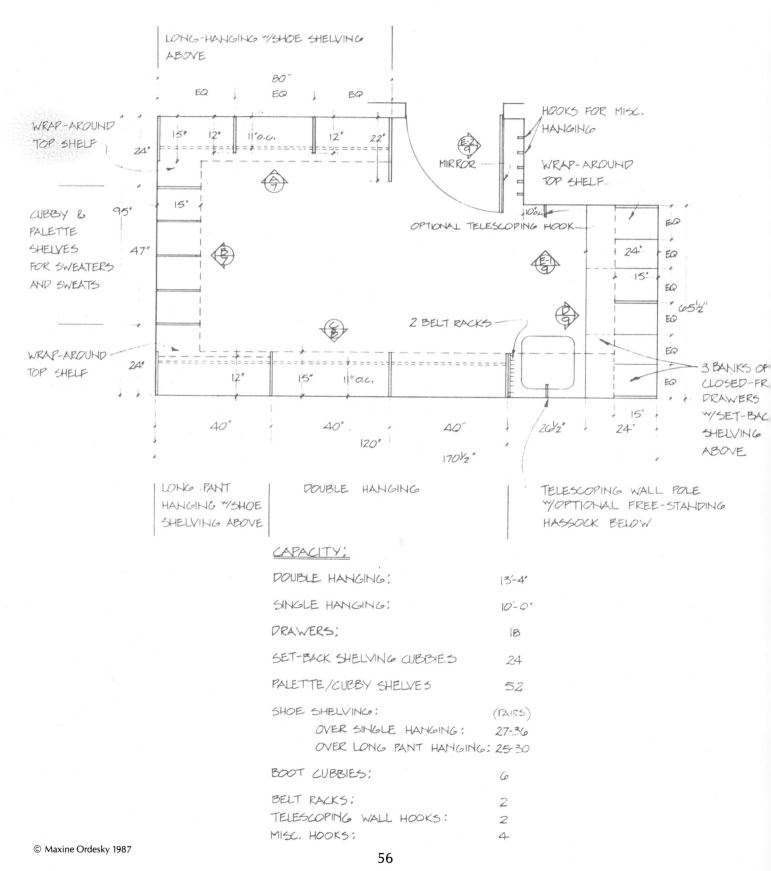

CAPACITY:

| | |
|---|---|
| DOUBLE HANGING: | 13'-4' |
| SINGLE HANGING: | 10'-0' |
| DRAWERS: | 18 |
| SET-BACK SHELVING CUBBIES | 24 |
| PALETTE/CUBBY SHELVES | 52 |
| SHOE SHELVING: | (PAIRS) |
| OVER SINGLE HANGING: | 27-36 |
| OVER LONG PANT HANGING: | 25-30 |
| BOOT CUBBIES: | 6 |
| BELT RACKS: | 2 |
| TELESCOPING WALL HOOKS: | 2 |
| MISC. HOOKS: | 4 |

The blueprint (left) and the photographs on this page all illustrate the same woman's walk-in closet. Ordesky's plan shows just how carefully she considers and designs to accommodate her client's specific needs. The photo on the right shows a wall of pull-out pallets for single sweater and shirt storage, a tall hanging rod for daytime dresses with shelves for hats above, and a lower hanging rod for suits, with shoe shelves above.

The pull-out pallets are a device that Ordesky favors because, since only one item fits on each pallet, wrinkling and clutter are eliminated. The hanging garments clear the floor by 2 or 3 inches, (5 to 8 centimeters) to bring them as close to eye level as possible.

*Lois Ellen Frank/Design: Maxine Ordesky, Beverly Hills, California*

The generous cubbies in this woman's closet (bottom left) keep her collection of handbags on display and within easy reach. The drawers below the cubbies are lined and partitioned to hold folded items and accessories. The top left-hand drawer is equipped with a lock and is used to store jewelry.

The top drawer (bottom right) is partitioned to accommodate rolled belts, each in its own compartment; the next drawer is designed to hold scarves, stoles, and gloves.

*Lois Ellen Frank/Design: Maxine Ordesky, Beverly Hills, California*

*Lois Ellen Frank/Design: Maxine Ordesky, Beverly Hills, California*

# A Man's Walk-In Closet

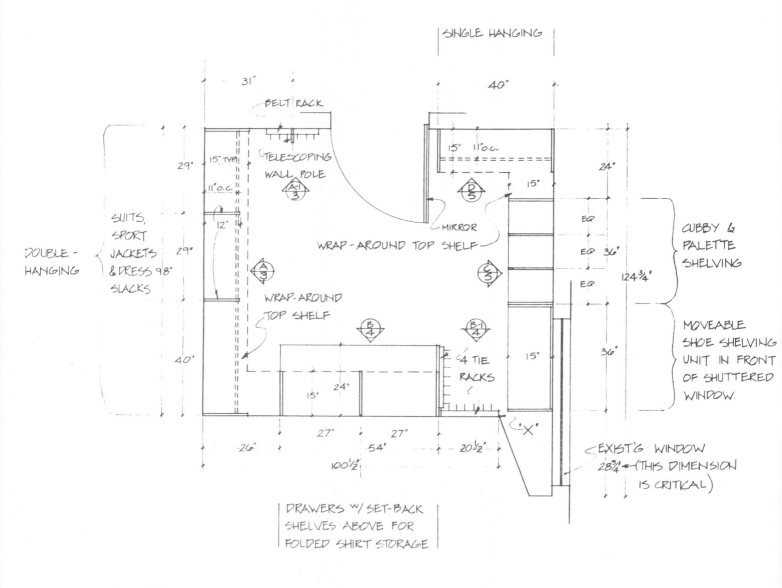

SINGLE HANGING

31"

BELT RACK

40"

TELESCOPING
WALL POLE

A-1
3

15" 11"o.c.

D
5

15"

24"

29"

15" TYP.

11"o.c.

12"

MIRROR

SUITS,
SPORT
JACKETS
& DRESS
SLACKS

29"

A
3

98"

WRAP-AROUND TOP SHELF

EQ

EQ 36"

EQ

CUBBY &
PALETTE
SHELVING

124¾"

DOUBLE -
HANGING

WRAP-AROUND
TOP SHELF

C
5

MOVEABLE
SHOE SHELVING
UNIT IN FRONT
OF SHUTTERED
WINDOW.

40"

B
4

B-1
4

4 TIE
RACKS

15"

36"

15"

24"

27"       27"

26"

54"

20½"

"X"

EXIST'G WINDOW
28¾" (THIS DIMENSION
IS CRITICAL)

100½"

DRAWERS w/ SET-BACK
SHELVES ABOVE FOR
FOLDED SHIRT STORAGE

CAPACITY:

| | |
|---|---|
| DOUBLE HANGING: | 16'-4" |
| SINGLE HANGING: | 3'-4" |
| DRAWERS: | 12 |
| SET-BACK SHELVES FOR SHIRTS STACKED. | |
| 1 HIGH: | 36 |
| 2 HIGH: | 72 |
| 3 HIGH: | 108 |

CUBBY & PALETTE SHELVING:  16 & 36 = 52

SHOE SHELVING:
OVER SINGLE-HANGING: 12-20 PRS.
IN FRONT OF WINDOW: 52-60 PRS.

| | |
|---|---|
| TIE RACKS: | 4 |
| BELT RACKS: | 1 |
| TELESCOPING POLE: | 1 |

*Lois Ellen Frank/Design: Maxine Ordesky, Beverly Hills, California*

**The blueprint (facing page) and the photographs on this page illustrate a man's walk-in closet. The photograph (left) shows double hanging for jackets and trousers, open shelves for sweaters, and closed, partitioned drawers for folded items and accessories.**

*Lois Ellen Frank/Design: Maxine Ordesky, Beverly Hills, California*

**This closet (left) was designed for a busy lawyer. He travels a lot and therefore, requires ample storage for folded shirts that can be easily tucked into a suitcase. Ordesky designed a pull-out pallet unit that can hold 108 shirts, neatly folded in anticipation of the next trip. To the left of the unit is hanging storage with a shoe shelf above; to the right of the unit is more shoe shelving. A high shelf overhead holds awkward items, including luggage.**

# A Walk-In For A Couple

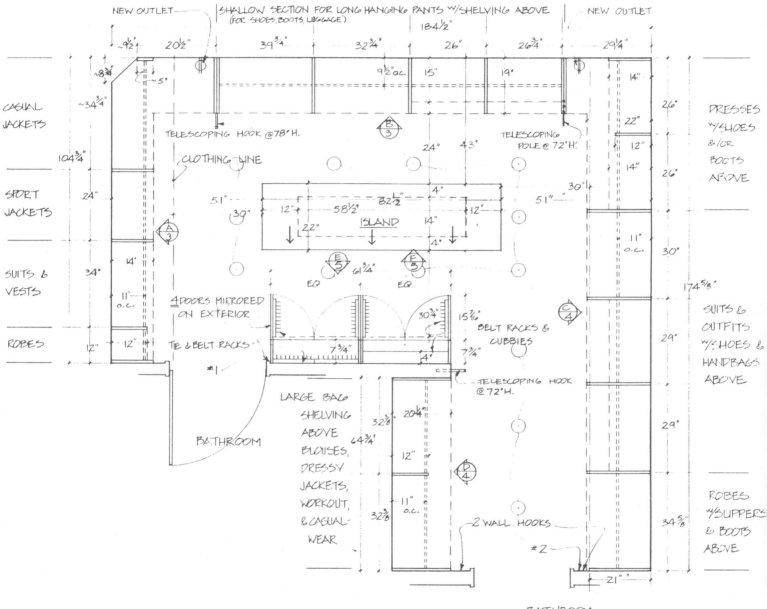

CAPACITIES

### HIS

| | OLD | NEW |
|---|---|---|
| CASUAL JACKETS | 51" | 69½" |
| SPORT JACKETS | 47" | 48" |
| SUITS & VESTS | 55" | 68" |
| SLACKS | 72" | 72½" |
| ROBES | — | 12" |
| SHOES | 32 PRS | 31 PRS |
| TIES | 6 RACKS (144) | 7 RACKS (168) |
| BELTS | 30 | 30 |

### HERS

| | OLD | NEW |
|---|---|---|
| NIGHTGOWNS & ROBES | 32" | 34½" |
| SUITS & OUTFITS | 86" | 88" |
| DRESSES | 50" | 52" |
| SLACKS | 40" | 52" |
| BLOUSES & DRESSY JACKETS | 47" | 64¾" |
| WORKOUT & CASUALWEAR | 48" | 64¾" |
| BELTS: ROLLED | | 84 |
| HANGING | ~170 | ~120 |
| SHOES | ~130 | ~107 |
| BOOTS | ~18 | 14 |
| HANDBAGS | 65 | 72-90 |
| DRAWERS | ~15 | 17 |
| SWEATER SHELVES | 3 | 4 SHELVES, 8 CUBBIES |

LUGGAGE & MISC. ON FIXED TOP SHELF: 38'

This walk-in closet was created for a couple who previously had separate closets. Although the closet is large, its total area is smaller than the total of the two closets the couple had before, so Ordesky had to conserve space whenever possible.

A wall unit contains small cubbies that hold rolled belts and costume jewelry. A center island has lined and partitioned drawers. It was designed to take up as little floor space as possible. "If the island were any larger," Ordesky says, "there wouldn't be enough room to walk around in the closet." The island's storage space is augmented by a shelving unit that is suspended from the ceiling above it.

The couple has separate bathrooms, each of which opens into the closet. Ordesky chose to use the space nearest the bathroom doors as dressing areas, complete with places for robes and slippers. This also allows the couple to dress at the same time, for they are on opposite sides of the closet and not in each other's way.

*These photographs show the final result of the blueprint on the previous pages. This unit (left) of very small cubbies was created especially to hold the woman's collection of ornate designer belts.*

*Here is an illustration (bottom left) of Ordesky's knack for packing a lot of storage into a fairly small space. Note the three shelving units for shoes, the tall, narrow cubbies for boots, the hanging rods at various heights, and the shelves for folded sweaters.*

Lois Ellen Frank/Design: Maxine Ordesky, Beverly Hills, California

Lois Ellen Frank/Design: Maxine Ordesky, Beverly Hills, California

*Ordesky found a way to use every inch of vertical space in this closet (below) by including hanging rods, shelves for shoe storage, and tall, narrow cubbies to hold the woman's collection of tote bags. The partitions between the cubbies can be removed to create another flat shelf, if needed. Notice that only one of each shoe is visible. Ordesky has found that the most space efficient way to store shoes is heel to heel, and she designs deeper shelves to accommodate this whenever she can.*

Lois Ellen Frank/Design: Maxine Ordesky, Beverly Hills, California

**Simple built-in shelves (above) hold folded sweaters and hats.**

**The man's section (below) has hanging rods at several heights for shirts, jackets, and trousers. Note the rod near the top right of the photo, where empty hangers are kept until they are needed.**

Lois Ellen Frank/Design: Maxine Ordesky, Beverly Hills, California

Lois Ellen Frank/Design: Maxine Ordesky, Beverly Hills, California

# A Baby's Closet

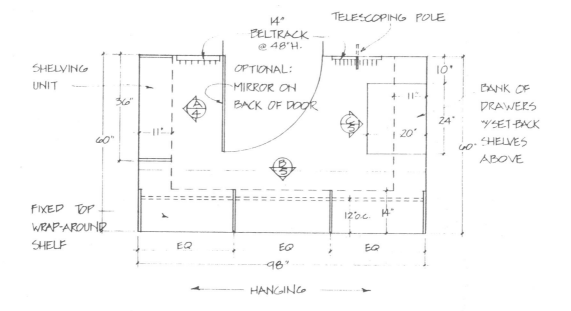

*Lois Ellen Frank/Design: Maxine Ordesky, Beverly Hills, California*

*Lois Ellen Frank/Design: Maxine Ordesky, Beverly Hills, California*

**The little girl's toys (above) stored on the shelves above the drawers, lend color and warmth to the closet.**

**This little girl's closet (blueprint at left, and photograph above) has several hanging rods close together, designed to hold tiny clothes. As the child grows, the rods can be moved, or even removed to accommodate larger garments. Some of the rods can be replaced with shelves, as the child's clothing needs change. The closed drawers hold folded items, and the shelves above the drawers can be used for clothes or toys.**

# A Child's Closet

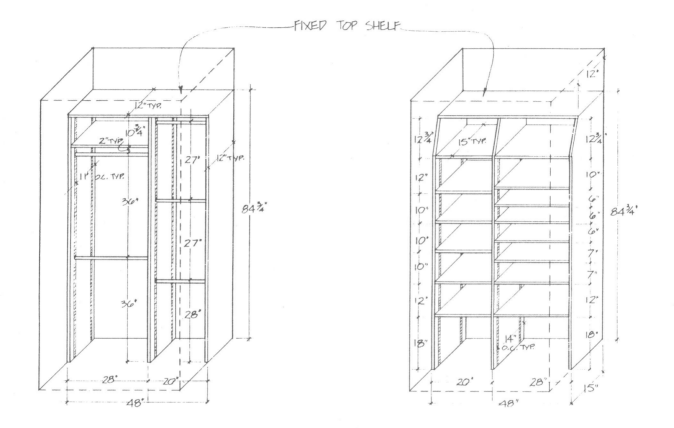

<u>NOTE</u>: CLOSET DOORS TO HAVE A BELT RACK (EACH DOOR) MOUNTED @ 48".

<u>CAPACITIES:</u>

| | |
|---|---|
| HANGING | 9'-8" |
| SHELVING | 31 RUNNING FEET |
| BELT RACKS | 2 |

OR, CLIENT OPTION: ONLY 1 BELT RACK & 1 DOOR MIRROR

The blueprint (left) and photograph (above) show a little boy's closet designed to be fully adjustable. The original plans called for the closet to contain nothing but shelves, but during the design process the mother changed her mind and asked that hanging storage be added as well. Now, rods are low enough to let the child reach and hang his own clothes, and they can be raised as the child grows. A bookshelf unit next to the closet has a countertop for folding and drawers underneath.

"The entire closet is geared to accommodate the child," says Ordesky. "He can reach everything, which makes a child feel he can do things for himself."

The shelves in the closet (right) hold a combination of folded clothing and toys, all visible and many within the child's reach.

*Sweaters on pull-out shelves in this man's closet (right) are easy to keep neat and organized. The narrow pull-out shelves eliminate the need to rummage through piles of sweaters to find the one you want.*

*Partitions (below) keep drawers neat while allowing easy access to the items within.*

# Personalized, But Flexible

The very best closets all share certain characteristics—they're custom-designed to suit the needs of their owners (even if they're accessorized with store-bought equipment), and they're flexible. The closet arrangement that seems ideal for your needs this year may not suit you five years from now, for your wardrobe and tastes may have changed. "Everything in my closets is adjustable," says Ordesky. "The hanging rods can be moved or taken out, the shelves can be moved up or down on side tracks, and some of the partitions between cubbies can be removed to turn the area into a flat shelf."

The experts also take care to design features that make the closet organization as easy to maintain as possible. Neatness and organization are the key to any storage system, but they have to be easy to keep up or the owner won't bother. Partitioned drawers, single-sweater pallets, pull-out drawers, and various kinds of cubbies are all natural outgrowths of the old-fashioned but ever true adage, "a place for everything, and everything in its place." This is much easier to adhere to if "a place for everything" is clearly defined, easy to reach, and enhances the area's overall look. As these photographs and plans have shown, the days of tossing everything into a closet and then hoping you can force the door shut behind you are over. Instead, it is time to examine the ways that a professional closet designer's expertise can make your life easier and keep your clothing in good shape at the same time.

Lois Ellen Frank/Design: Maxine Ordesky, Beverly Hills, California

*These pull-out pallets for sweaters and shirts (above) are wonderful and organized. Each pallet holds only one sweater or several shirts, which keeps each item easy to see and wrinkle free.*

# The Architect's Solutions

Before a closet can be designed, built, or rebuilt, its problems and the needs of the people who will be using it must be taken into consideration. During the designing phase, a professional will find out precisely what must be stored in the closet, measure the closet carefully, then sketch possible solutions to the client's storage problems. Once the drawing has been made, it is examined by both the client and the professional, so that both can decide if it offers the best possible solutions and meets all of the client's needs. The drawing will be refined and altered until it is as close to perfect as possible. Once the drawing is complete, work on the closet itself can begin.

The blueprints on the following pages show basic designs for a woman's closet, a man's closet, a family room closet, a linen closet, and a child's closet. All are designed for the average closet space. You should be able to adapt some of the ideas here to your own space and storage considerations.

Lois Ellen Frank/Design: Maxine Ordesky, Beverly Hills, California

*This man's closet (above) demonstrates the space-saving technique of using several hanging rods at different heights. All kinds of shirts are hung, eliminating the need for a dresser. Shoes are at eye level, for easy accessibility.*

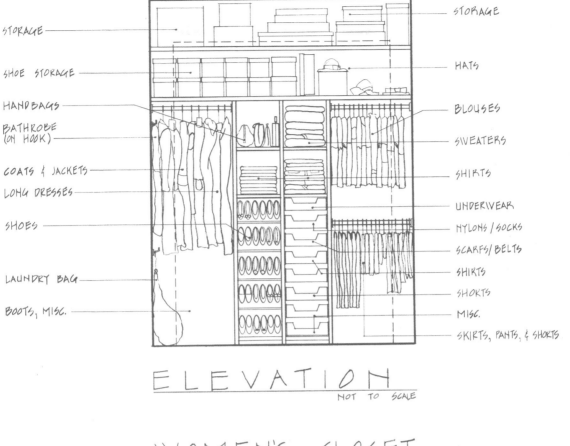

STORAGE

SHOE STORAGE

HANDBAGS

BATHROBE
(ON HOOK)

COATS & JACKETS

LONG DRESSES

SHOES

LAUNDRY BAG

BOOTS, MISC.

STORAGE

HATS

BLOUSES

SWEATERS

SHIRTS

UNDERWEAR

NYLONS / SOCKS

SCARFS / BELTS

SHIRTS

SHORTS

MISC.

SKIRTS, PANTS, & SHORTS

ELEVATION
NOT TO SCALE

WOMEN'S CLOSET

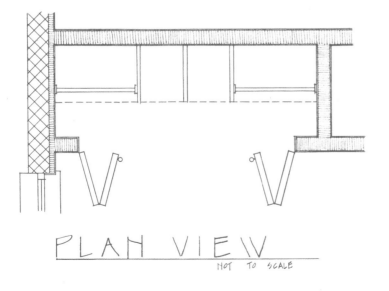

PLAN VIEW
NOT TO SCALE

This woman's closet must hold a complete wardrobe. A woman wants everything in view, so she can choose her clothes easily each morning. The solution is a combination of hanging and folded storage. One side of the closet is for long storage, such as dresses, and the other holds two hanging rods, one above the other, for shorter items. Shoes are kept on narrow shoe shelves, with a taller shelf above for handbags. Pull-out shelves next to the shoes hold folded items. A high shelf is used to store out-of-season items, and the floor space is kept clear to hold a laundry bag and to serve as temporary storage, when needed.

Some men want the closet to double as a dresser, so this design has many shelves to hold folded items. One side has only one hanging rod, to accommodate long items; the other side is double-hung to hold shorter items. Shoes are on shelves, which frees the floor space for temporary storage as needed. Little-used and awkwardly shaped items are stored on high top shelves.

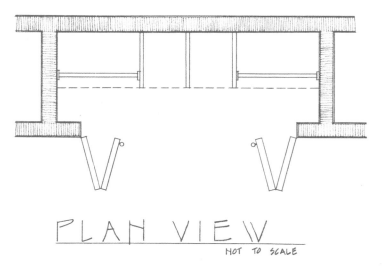

PLAN VIEW
NOT TO SCALE

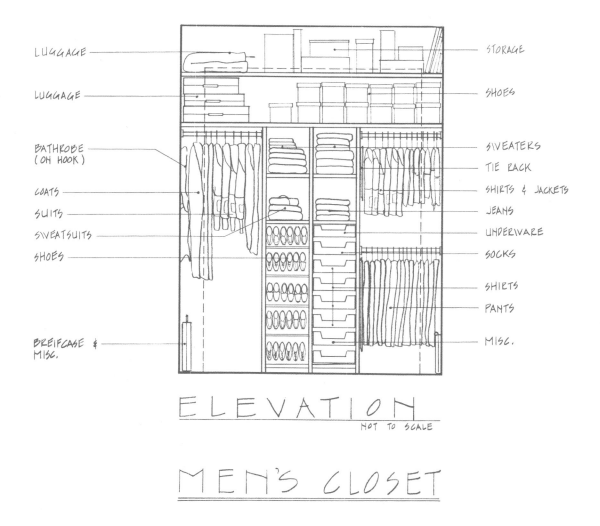

LUGGAGE — STORAGE

LUGGAGE — SHOES

BATHROBE (ON HOOK) — SWEATERS

TIE RACK

COATS — SHIRTS & JACKETS

SUITS — JEANS

SWEATSUITS — UNDERWARE

SHOES — SOCKS

SHIRTS

PANTS

BREIFCASE & MISC. — MISC.

ELEVATION
NOT TO SCALE

MEN'S CLOSET

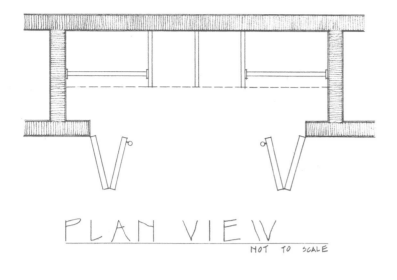

PLAN VIEW
NOT TO SCALE

The top priorities in a child's closet are safety and accessibility. The toys are stored on low shelves, so the child will not be tempted to climb for something beyond his reach. Everyday clothes are hung at the child's level, to encourage him to dress himself and to put his own clothes away. A laundry hamper is kept on the closet floor, below a shelf. All the shelves and rods are adjustable to change as the child grows up.

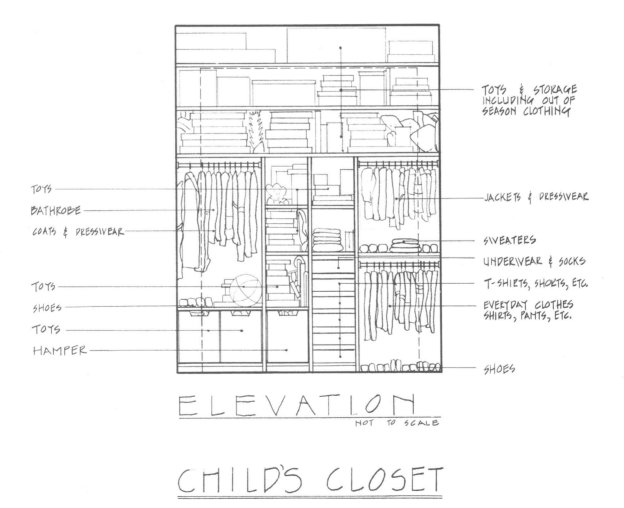

ELEVATION
NOT TO SCALE

CHILD'S CLOSET

This family room closet has to provide multipurpose storage for an entire family's hobby equipment, games, and personal items. To meet these needs, the closet is divided into different sized cubbies and shelves to accommodate various items. Tall, bulky items are stored in the large, open space on the lower left; video and audio cassettes are stored above them on shelves tailored to their size. Each family member has a pull-out box for small personal items.

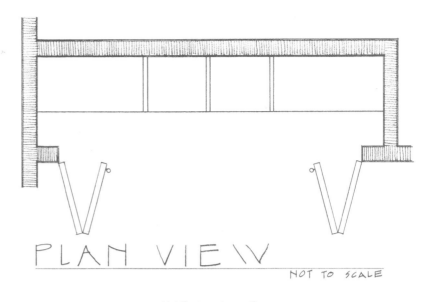

PLAN VIEW

NOT TO SCALE

NOT TO SCALE

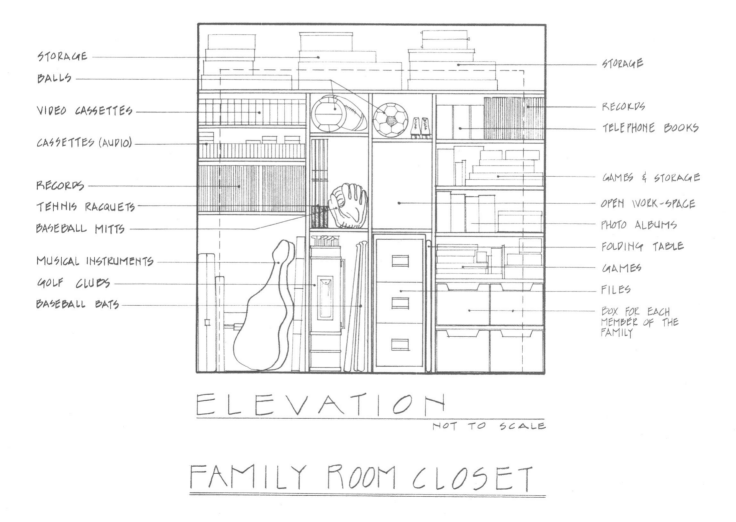

STORAGE
BALLS
VIDEO CASSETTES
CASSETTES (AUDIO)
RECORDS
TENNIS RACQUETS
BASEBALL MITTS
MUSICAL INSTRUMENTS
GOLF CLUBS
BASEBALL BATS

STORAGE
RECORDS
TELEPHONE BOOKS
GAMES & STORAGE
OPEN WORK-SPACE
PHOTO ALBUMS
FOLDING TABLE
GAMES
FILES
BOX FOR EACH MEMBER OF THE FAMILY

ELEVATION

NOT TO SCALE

FAMILY ROOM CLOSET

This tall, narrow linen closet must hold a variety of linen and laundry accessories, including bulky blankets and pillows. This problem can be solved by grouping the items by category and storing each type of item on separate shelves, to keep them all accessible. Seasonal items, such as blankets, are kept on the highest, least accessible shelves. Every inch of space is used in this closet—cleaning supplies are kept on the floor below the bottom shelf, and a fold-down ironing board is attached to the inside of the door.

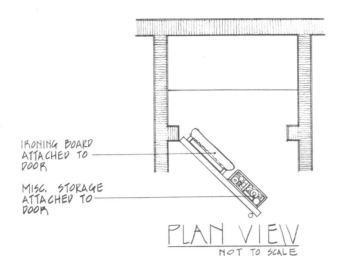

IRONING BOARD ATTACHED TO DOOR

MISC. STORAGE ATTACHED TO DOOR

PLAN VIEW
NOT TO SCALE

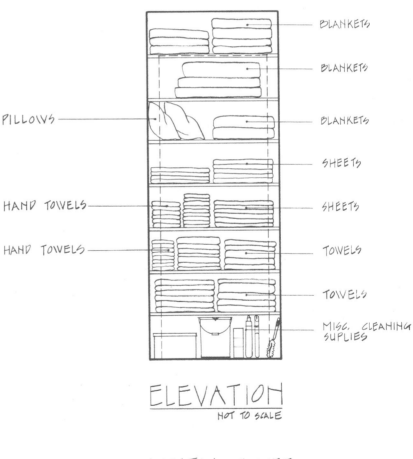

PILLOWS

HAND TOWELS

HAND TOWELS

BLANKETS

BLANKETS

BLANKETS

SHEETS

SHEETS

TOWELS

TOWELS

MISC. CLEANING SUPLIES

ELEVATION
NOT TO SCALE

LINEN CLOSET

# Chapter Five:
# CABINETS AND CUPBOARDS

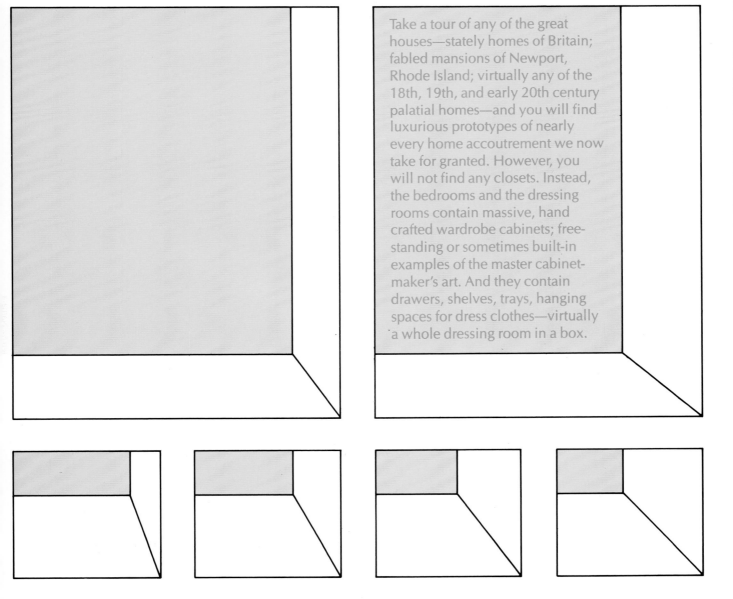

Take a tour of any of the great houses—stately homes of Britain; fabled mansions of Newport, Rhode Island; virtually any of the 18th, 19th, and early 20th century palatial homes—and you will find luxurious prototypes of nearly every home accoutrement we now take for granted. However, you will not find any closets. Instead, the bedrooms and the dressing rooms contain massive, hand crafted wardrobe cabinets; free-standing or sometimes built-in examples of the master cabinet-maker's art. And they contain drawers, shelves, trays, hanging spaces for dress clothes—virtually a whole dressing room in a box.

Today we are in the midst of a renaissance of the art of fine cabinetry. According to Mara Luben of the ICF New York design staff, "When artisans' skill and disciplined design are combined with the newest in manufacturing and assembly techniques, the results can be truly spectacular."

Even if you prefer traditional closets in your bedrooms and family areas, you will find that mastering the art of cabinet and cupboard storage will serve you well.

Richard Ross

**Left: The wall of this bedroom is an attractive combination of closed cabinet storage space and open bookshelves.**

*Below: The storage units in this room contribute to its distinctive elegance. In place of traditional closets and dressers, there are two freestanding clothing closets and a series of closed storage boxes. Open shelving is used as an accent and to lend an airier feeling to the space.*

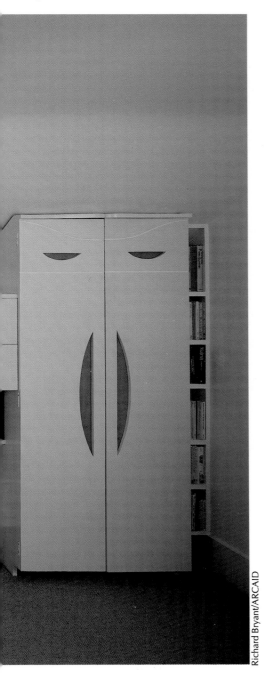

Richard Bryant/ARCAID

Jessica Strang/Design: Colin Forbes

*Above: This storage wall is ideal for a hallway or other long, narrow space. The front provides open shelving; the side offers a narrow cabinet and small drawers.*

# The Bedroom

Cupboard walls from Interlubke of Germany are storage units that become part of the architecture. From Italy, Boffi also illustrates how a mundane need for storage space can be transformed with elements possessing an architectural quality all their own. A room's proportions can be played with, spaces redefined, and rooms created within rooms.

Interlubke introduced the first Cupboard Wall in the mid-1960s. Since then, changes have been made in construction methods and installation systems, and the finishes and designs have grown in number, but the underlying principle has remained constant: the personalized integration of storage space into a room so beautifully that the room itself is enhanced.

*Above: A loft-style bed sits directly on top of a group of drawers. This arrangement takes up far less floor space than would a bed and a separate chest of drawers.*

*Facing page, top: This cupboard wall proves that storage need not only be practical; it can also aesthetically enhance a room.*

*Facing page, bottom: Two tall, narrow closets flank the bed and lend visual interest to an otherwise box-like room.*

*Left: This murphy-style bed folds up into a storage unit of drawers, cabinets, and shelves. When the bed is in use, the storage unit doubles as a bedside table.*

The height of the Cupboard Wall is dictated by the buyer. Single door units are added to accommodate the buyer's needs. And inside there are fixtures and fittings to meet every possible need, from storing the laundry to keeping shoes in perfect condition. All of the fittings may be moved up, down, and around to suit different situations. If space is at a premium, the gliding door wardrobe can run around corners without reducing accessibility or storage space. The Butterfly Door Cupboard is the newest and most unusual concept from Interlubke. In it, angled double doors zig-zag across a wall or bracket flat, open elements or conventional doors. The extra depth provided by the angle is perfect for gowns, furs, or bulky coats.

*Above: This unobtrusive cupboard wall is barely noticeable when its mirrored doors are closed. Here, it is opened to reveal the abundance of storage space concealed within.*

*Right: The versatility of cupboards is demonstrated by this design. When this unit is closed (near right), you see only an attractive wooden door that would complement any traditional-style decor. When it is opened (far right), you see the cleverly placed combination of cabinet, shelf and drawer space within.*

*Below: This cupboard wall combines high style with practicality. The enclosed drawers provide a space for more personal belongings, while the shelves serve as a showcase for collectibles.*

Atelier International Ltd.,/Courtesy William, Kent, Schoenfisch

Atelier International Ltd.,/Courtesy William, Kent, Schoenfisch

Atelier International Ltd.,/Courtesy William, Kent, Schoenfisch

*Left: This luxurious wall unit has a space for everything from shoes and accessories to suits and coats.*

*Below: This custom-fitted narrow chest of drawers can almost double the capacity of a cramped closet without wasting valuable floor space.*

© Robert Perron/S. Lasar

*Facing page: These drawers of varying depths can accommodate an entire wardrobe in a somewhat narrow area. When the doors are closed, the drawers are hidden from view.*

# The Kitchen

Because the kitchen is a center of activity in many homes—not only is it used for food storage and preparation, it is also a dining area, meeting place, telephone center, and sometimes a home office—it can be especially difficult to keep it clutter-free. But it is worth extra effort to keep it neat because a well organized kitchen space makes everyday tasks so much easier. By maximizing your kitchen's storage areas (usually cabinets and cupboards) you will be able to minimize the clutter.

The average kitchen has a great deal of potential storage space. Cabinet organizers, in the form of wire baskets that are fastened underneath shelves, or on walls, or that rest on top of shelves, are your best bet for clearing clutter off work surfaces. Horizontal organizers that rest on top of shelves allow you to stack different kinds of dishes on top of one another, separated by the wire shelf for easy access. Vertical organizers placed on shelves let you keep napkins, recipe cards, and other flat items neatly "filed." Undershelf organizers serve as extra shelves to hold folded towels, brown paper bags, or cookbooks. Narrow racks fastened to the walls or inner doors of a cabinet hold cleaning supplies and miscellaneous kitchen necessities, such as aluminum foil and plastic wrap. Canned goods can also be stored in these racks.

*Above: Take the time to think about the best ways to fulfill your storage needs. The drawer dividers shown here illustrate an ingenious yet simple solution to clutter.*

**Above: Take the time to maintain your storage areas. Grouping these canned goods according to type and frequency of use helps to keep this shelved cabinet neat and easy to use. Even the most elaborately designed storage system will be useless if you toss things in it haphazardly.**

**Left: A pegboard can eliminate the problem of awkwardly shaped items that are always falling over or blocking your way. A broom, mop, dustpan, and other items hang on the inside of a closet door—the ideal location for a pegboard—and are thus kept neatly out of the way until needed.**

James R. Levin

87

Jessica Strang/Consultant: Rosamund Julius

**Above: This eating area is surrounded by storage space, separating it from the kitchen. The closed doors of the cabinet wall conceal tableware, canned goods, pots, pans and an array of kitchen sundries.**

**Right: A kitchen cabinet can offer more than just storage space. This one conceals a "communication center" featuring a collapsible desk (complete with lamp) and a telephone. When not in use, the desk can be folded up into the cabinet.**

*Left: An arrangement of wire baskets and shelf systems turn a small utility closet into a commodious storage space. The shelves are placed at varying heights to allow room to store oversized items, such as the bucket shown.*

*Right: This closet has been customized for use as a china cabinet. Note the wine glasses hanging upside down from notched wooden bars at the top.*

© Robert Perron/Wine Rack: R. Phipps

Courtesy of Quakermaid

*Left: These swing-out shelf units pack a lot of storage into a little bit of space. In addition to conventional shelving inside the cabinet, the center unit rotates to reveal shelves on either side; the units on the right and left are built directly onto the inside of the cabinet doors.*

# Living Areas

The family room and living room are prime candidates for clutter, especially in households with children, who tend to let things lay where they have been dropped. But do not think that children are the only culprits; adults are frequently guilty of piling up magazines, newspapers, half-read books, records, tapes, needle-point-in-progress, paperwork, toys, paraphernalia for hobbies, unread mail, and other assorted (and difficult to classify) items in the living areas of a home. It seems that if an item does not fit easily into a particular category, it will wind up in the middle of a common living space. These living spaces support too many other activities to also accommodate items that need to be stored.

A built-in or freestanding cabinet or cupboard, divided into sections and shelves, is an attractive and practical solution to the problem. You can choose a cupboard that runs the length of a wall for an abundance of storage space, or you can select a more compact

© Peter Paige/Tom Gass

*Right: This cabinet combines slots and shelves to allow for organization of articles such as bags and magazines. Its angled upper area also serves as a surface to jot down phone memos.*

*Facing page: These shelves serve a double purpose in this restful study: They both organize books and showcase other precious objects.*

model to give you just a bit of extra room. You can choose a unit with doors to enclose the contents, or one with some open space from which to display collections and memorabilia. And, because cabinets and cupboards are available in a wide range of finishes, you should have no trouble finding one to complement your existing decor.

As with any kind of storage, carefully consider what you need from the cabinet before you choose it. A wide variety of shelf and section options allow you to organize the contents several ways. A unit with adjustable shelves will allow you to group similarly sized possessions together, regardless of ownership. Or, with a sectioned cupboard, you might prefer to group items by category rather than size; designate one area of the cupboard for books, another for magazines, a third for board games, a fourth for uncategorized items. If these methods of organization do not suit your needs, consider the terri-torial approach. Allot each member of the family his or her own storage space (each one should be of roughly equal size to prevent squabbles among siblings) and explain that the space is the new home of those things normally found lying about the family room. Encourage everyone to sort through their stored items periodically and throw away items that have outlived their usefulness. Make sure they understand that the cabinet, like all closets, is not a catch-all for junk.

**Above: Open shelving doubles as a display case for the handsome collection of books it houses.**

*Facing page, top: Books and other prized possessions are displayed neatly in this wall unit composed of shelves of different sizes.*

*Facing page, bottom: A combination of open and closed storage areas makes this wall unit striking. Note the fold-down table topped by shallow shelves for papers and files.*

Above: Storage spaces can be nearly invisible, as illustrated by lowered louvered doors of this wall unit. The doors allow air to circulate to minimize dampness and dust inside the closet.

Above: Here's the same room, with the louvered doors raised to expose the drawers, shelves, and electronic equipment hidden within.

Facing page, top: This unusual solution to space problems more than doubles the storage area of a single space. Instead of using only the area above the drawers as storage space, this approach turns shelves sideways.

Facing page: Here is an outstanding example of a high-tech storage solution. The sleekly modern space pictured in these two photographs is filled with boxes, cabinets, drawers, and grids. Note how they are integrated into the design of the room (left). To add visual interest, small, differently-shaped cabinet doors are built into the wall. These spaces can accommodate hundreds of possessions without a hint of clutter.

Chapter Six:

# ATTENTION
# TO
# DETAIL

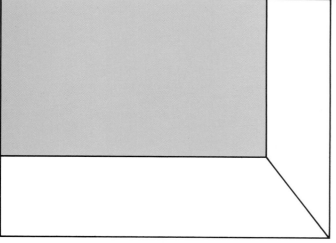

It is not enough to have the perfect storage system—you also need to store your clothes properly in order to get the most out of the systems you have installed.

# Storage Guidelines

Careful storage makes an enormous difference in the appearance and life-span of your clothes. Here are some guidelines you should bear in mind before putting your clothes in any closet:

—Hanging up your clothes while they are still warm from the heat of your body allows the creases to fall out. But do not put them immediately in the closet as soon as you have placed them on the hangers. Let them air out on a shower rod for a few minutes.

—Empty all pockets of keys, loose change, and so on before putting clothes away. The weight of these items can pull fabric permanently out of shape.

—Brush your clothes to remove lint or dust before putting them away.

—Get in the habit of mending tears or missing buttons as soon as you notice them; you will spare yourself some unpleasant surprises later.

—As you place items in your closet, make sure that sleeves are

straight, lapels are smooth, etc., to prevent wrinkling.

—Hang your clothes so they all face in the same direction. Group your clothes into categories, such as business and informal or sports wear. Make sure the clothes are not jammed up against one another—there should be enough space to allow air to circulate around them.

**Left:** *A traditional but always effective solution to clutter; the simple "captain's bed" with a deep drawer.*

**Above:** *This small laundry room equipped with a linen closet has been designed to use every bit of space efficiently. Storage areas for towels and a small table for supplies keep things attractively organized.*

Bill Rothschild/Design: Lee Napolitano

© Robert Perron/R. Phipps

# Using Hangers

Courtesy Lillian Vernon Corp.

Although nearly all articles of clothing can be folded to stay neat in a minimum amount of space, you might prefer to hang certain items. Follow these guidelines to keep clothes looking their best:

—Double barred wooden hangers are excellent for men's suits because they are strong enough to carry the weight of a three-piece suit. Fold the trousers over the lower bar and arrange the jacket and vest on the top bar. Plastic or wooden hangers that are gently curved to match the contours of your shoulders and back are ideal for coats and jackets. Soft padded hangers are the best choice for dresses because they are less likely to pull delicate fabrics out of shape.

—Clamp or clip hangers are best for skirts—they force the skirt to hang straight from the waistband making it less likely to stretch than it would be if hung from the fabric loops sewn inside the waistband. It is okay to hang more than one skirt from clamp or clip hangers, as long as you can do so without bunching or wrinkling the waistbands.

—Whatever hanger you use, make sure it does not extend beyond the shoulders of a garment. If it pokes into the sleeve, it will leave a bump.

*Facing page: A ladder provides access to the top shelves. Note the efficient use of baskets and shelves and their easy accessibility.*

*Above: These sweater and shoe bags conserve space by storing normally bulky items in a narrow, vertical space.*

# HANGING TECHNIQUES

Here are some techniques that will keep your clothes in shape.

## Jackets

Empty the pockets and make sure the jacket is unbuttoned to allow air to circulate inside. The center of the collar should lie against the crook of the hanger, and the shoulders should be level so the jacket hangs straight.

## Trousers

Remove the belt and empty the pockets. Hang the trousers over the bar at a point about six inches above the knees. If you are using a double-barred hanger, the trousers must be centered to prevent creasing. Line up the inseam and outside seam of each leg to keep the front crease in place.

## Skirts

Use a clamp or clip hanger, making sure that the waistband is lying smooth and flat.

## Dresses

Soft padded hangers are the best choice for dresses made of delicate fabrics. Fasten buttons and zippers to keep the fabric from sagging under its own weight. Puffed sleeves should be filled with tissue paper, and cuffs should lie flat against the skirt.

Hang strapless long dresses from the waistband, as well as any dress in which the skirt's weight might pull the bodice out of shape, such as dresses with "spaghetti" shoulder straps and long dresses with heavy skirts.

Courtesy Lillian Vernon Corp.

Bill Rothschild/"Closet Systems"

**Facing page: This sturdy hanger keeps five pairs of pants in place and protects them from wrinkling.**

**Above: This multi-level closet keeps clothes neat and within reach. Note hanging bars for pants.**

## Jeans

You can avoid a crease on the front and back of the legs by folding jeans lengthwise so that the back pockets press against each other and draping them over a hanger.

## Coats

Empty the pockets and hang a coat as you would a jacket. Never hang coats by the loop at the back of the neck for any length of time—it pulls the coat out of shape.

## Hats

Stack one hat inside the other. If you wear hair mousse or spray, protect the outside of the stacked hats by lining the inside of each with tissue paper before storing.

## Furs

Use a broad-shouldered padded hanger to support fur coats and jackets. Make certain that the fur has plenty of room to itself to keep it from being crushed or matted by pressure from other garments. Cover the fur with a loose cloth or cloth bag to protect it from dust. Some furs, such as fox, shed for a while when new—a cloth bag prevents stray hairs from getting on the rest of your clothes.

Jessica Strang/ Architect: Theo Crosby

*Above: All clothes are accessible when placed on moving "coat-room-style" racks like those installed here.*

*Facing page: This closet maximizes the capacity of a small space with shelves for foldable items and a space below for larger possessions.*

# FOLDING

Not all garments should be hung up. Fold anything that might stretch out of shape, such as sweaters and any knit garments. You may even prefer to fold many items that can be hung, because folded, stacked garments take up a minimal amount of closet space.

## *Shirts and Blouses*

Here is an easy, seven-step method for folding shirts and blouses.

1) Fasten the top and middle buttons to keep the sides in position, then lay the shirt face down.
2) Fold one side in a third of the way toward the back.
3) Bring the sleeve on the folded side over to rest on the fold, laying it straight from shoulder to shirt-tails.
4) Repeat steps 2 and 3 on the second side. The second sleeve will lie partly over the first.
5) Fold the tails of the shirt up over the cuffs.
6) Fold the shirt crosswise so that the end of the shirt reaches the lower edge of the collar.
7) Place the shirt face up on a shelf.

After they are folded, silk blouses and men's formal shirts should be wrapped in white tissue paper to protect them from dust.

Courtesy Lillian Vernon Corp.

## Sweaters

You can fold a sweater as you would a shirt, or you can follow the instructions given below. This fold makes it possible for the sweater to lay flatter on a shelf or in a drawer. Cashmere and other delicate sweaters should always be folded this way to minimize wrinkling.

1) Lay the sweater face down. Fold the first sleeve across the back.
2) Fold the second sleeve across the back, over the first sleeve.
3) Bring the bottom of the sweater to the inside edge of the yoke.
4) Store the sweater face upward.

By folding your clothes properly, you will help keep your closet neat while making sure that your clothes always look fresh and ready to wear.

*Facing page: A freestanding shelf unit holds dozens of items and takes up a minimum of floor space. It can be placed in a closet or used in a room as an open storage/display area.*

*Left: Garment bags can help maximize space while protecting clothes from dust and moths. Note the space saving shoe bag and the shelf divisions in the center bag.*

Like almost everything else, neatness is a habit. And habits are learned by repetition, until they become unconscious acts. In a child, neatness is far more than a virtue. By teaching your young child the habit of neatness, you save yourself the hours many parents spend ordering adolescents to "clean up your room!" Your 12-year-old will react far more positively to that request if he has been picking up after himself since early childhood.

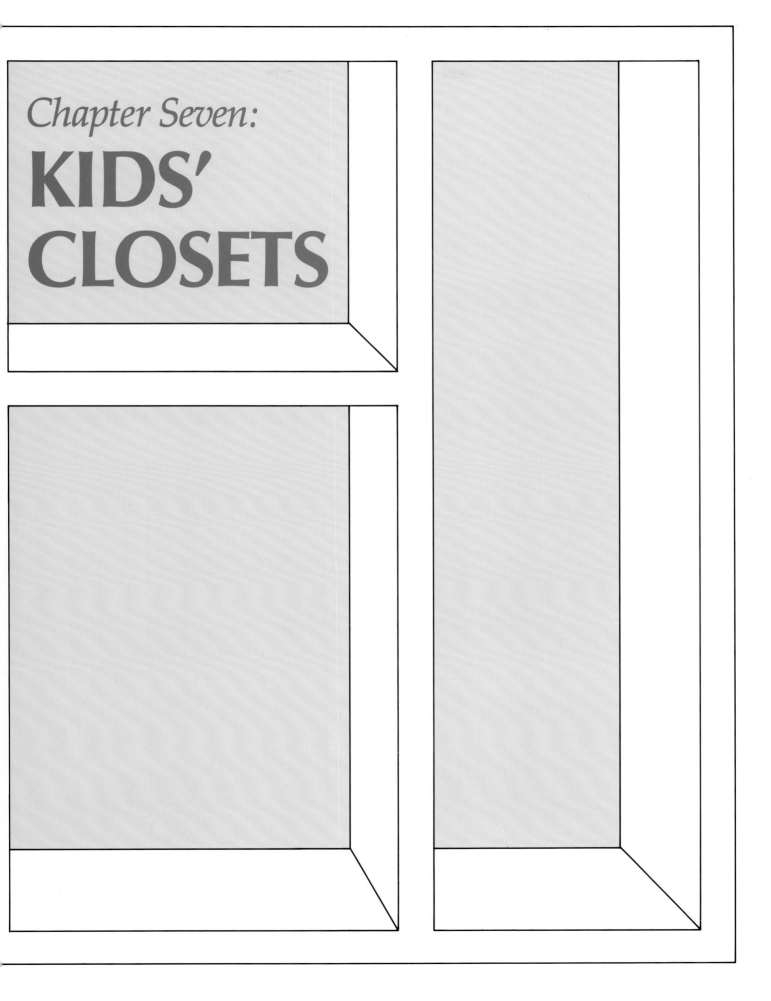

# Chapter Seven:
# KIDS' CLOSETS

Although you cannot reasonably expect a very young child to take full responsibility for his room and his belongings, you *can* expect him to develop the habit of putting his toys away when he is through with them, and of placing his dirty clothes in the hamper and his clean clothes in the closet. He will be able to do this, however, only if you provide him with storage systems that are appropriate to his size and level of coordination.

Parents cannot ask a 3-foot tall kindergartener to hang clothes on a 6-foot tall pole, or to wrestle open a full size, heavy wooden dresser drawer. However, parents can avoid problems entirely by scaling storage systems down to child size and tailoring them to a child's specific needs.

According to Judith Miley of Clairson International, "A child's closet should contain shelf-and-rod combinations in a bilevel ar-

rangement for sportswear, separates, or child-sized dresses and coats, and several shelves for folded clothing, linens, toys, and games. You might even include a hamper and a lightweight drawer system for socks, pajamas, and toys. All these storage components fit into the closet, which opens up space in the room that was once occupied by a toy chest or bureau. Also, the child can reach everything easily.

Jessica Strang/Design: Farrow

"This makes it possible for your youngster to care for his own clothing and possessions. You are creating eye level compartments that are distinctly intended for certain uses. Racks of hooks invite hats, jackets, and backpacks.

"Kids love it, and so do their parents. Out-of-season or dress-up clothing can occupy the upper level shelf-and-rod, so young children are more likely to select appropriate school or play outfits that are not mixed in with clothing the parents would not allow them to wear for a particular occasion. By selecting their own outfits and deciding where clothing and games should be kept, children learn to make decisions and to feel in control of a portion of their lives. It is a very positive thing for both the child and parent."

As you plan your child's closet, remember that keeping shelves at the child's eye level will encourage him to put his toys away. Consider placing shelves on adjustable brackets that can be raised as the child grows. For safety's sake, do not store toys on shelves that your child can see but not reach. He might be tempted to climb on the shelf to reach a favorite toy.

*Facing page: The mirrored doors of this wide closet make the room seem larger. The area above is used to display favorite toys.*

*Right: A child's loft bed is perched atop capacious shelves and drawers.*

© Karen Bussolini/Design: Gilvarg/Epstein

If closet space is very limited, consider hanging vinyl coated wire wall grids with hooks to hold jackets, scarves, hats, and items waiting to be more properly stored. Children have so many favorite little things (miniature cars, building blocks, puzzle pieces, etc.) that you must consider using some unconventional storage methods as well. Here are a few suggestions.

—Three-tiered wire baskets intended to store vegetables are lightweight, inexpensive, and readily available in department stores. They can be hung from the underside of a shelf and used to collect small items that might otherwise stay on the floor.

— Paint large, empty coffee cans bright colors, or cover them with construction paper, then stack them against a wall. Their cheerful, colorful appearance will encourage your child to store small toys in them.

— Clear plastic boxes let the child see what's inside. These can be stacked inside a closet.

— Small toys and games can be placed in drawstring bags and hung from grids for easy access.

You will get even more out of a child-tailored storage space if you apply the same principles you use when reorganizing other closets in the house. Old, abandoned toys and games should be discarded.

*Left: Unique beds have built-in, yet flexible storage that will grow with children. The shelves allow children to create an ever-changing display of their collections and toys.*

PEOPLE
ROBOTS
CRAYONS
GOS
LOREN'S TOOLS
KITCHEN-WARE
BIG TRAIN
SM
TR

*Above: A changing table provides ample storage for and easy access to diapers and clothes. Stuffed animals can also be positioned on top or hidden within drawers.*

*Above: Colorful bins of varying sizes make ideal catchalls for children's toys, supplies, and projects-in-progress. To minimize clutter and potential confusion, label them clearly and store them on easily accessible shelves, so that even young children can find and use them.*

Courtesy Lillian Vernon Corp.

Courtesy Home Magazine/ Photo: Jeff McNamara

**Above: A large, soft-sided box makes an ideal toy chest for young children. Avoid toy boxes with lids, which may fall as children reach inside.**

**Left: situated at the perfect height for a child, the closet system has both open and closed storage components that avoid clutter and offer easy access to toys, too. The child's loft-type bed above the closet is an added touch providing a unique design that extends space.**

© Peter Paige/Ari Bahat

**Above: This under-stair shelving is a clever way to utilize ordinarily wasted space.**

*Right: This simple closet is ideal for a growing child. Note generous shelf space on the right for toys and sporting goods.*

*Below: These boxes provide convenient under-bed storage without the trouble or expense of having a drawer built. Each box can be used for a different kind of possession, such as sweaters, toys, notebooks, and other necessary miscellany.*

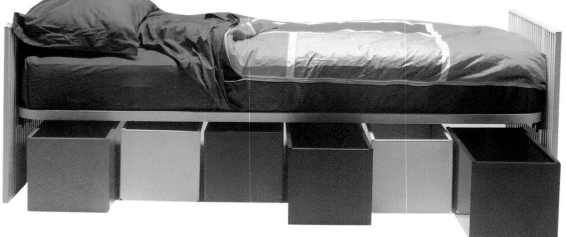

Courtesy Home Magazine/ Photo: Jeff McNamara

Biesse

*Below: Children are natural collectors, and a pegboard lets them display their collections without cluttering the room.*

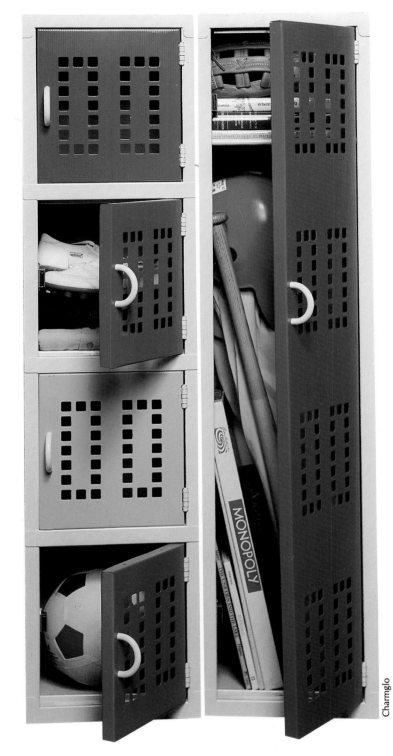

Charmglo

*Above: This freestanding locker-style storage unit is ideal for the budding athlete. The right-hand compartment holds tall items; the other sections hold books, gym equipment, and toys. The holes in the doors allow air to circulate within to minimize mustiness.*

*Above: A storage unit such as this one allows a child to take an active role in storing his/her own clothes and toys. Here, a colorful collection of shoes sits neatly on shelves, while a stuffed-animal collection is snugly contained in an open basket nearby.*

Jessica Strang

Jessica Strang/ Design: Sonny Howson

*Above: Sometimes storage solutions have to be custom-fitted to a space to be truly effective. In this case, a raised platform allows drawers to be placed between the two levels of a room.*

Richard Bryant/ARCAID

*Right: This child's bed has enclosed sides to keep the youngster safe. It sits compactly on top of storage drawers whose unusual design echoes the angularity of the window panes.*

121

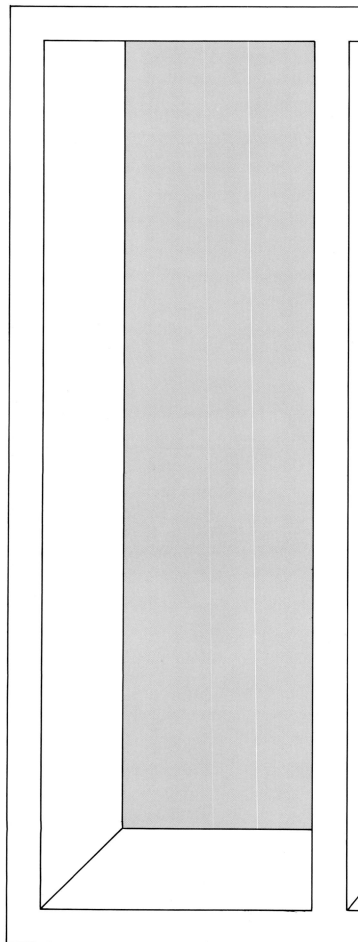
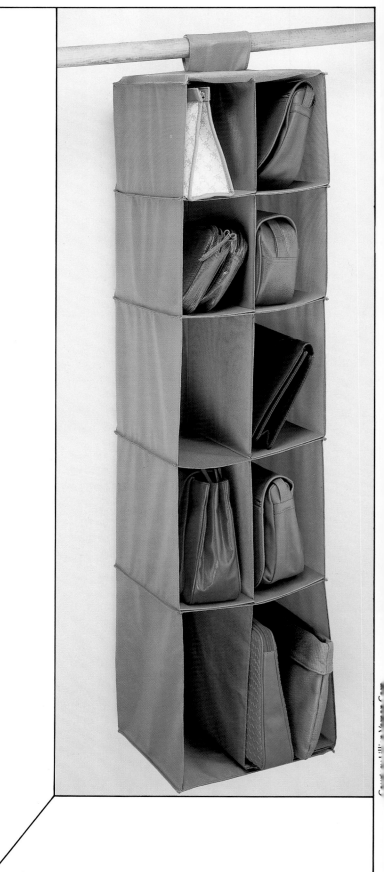

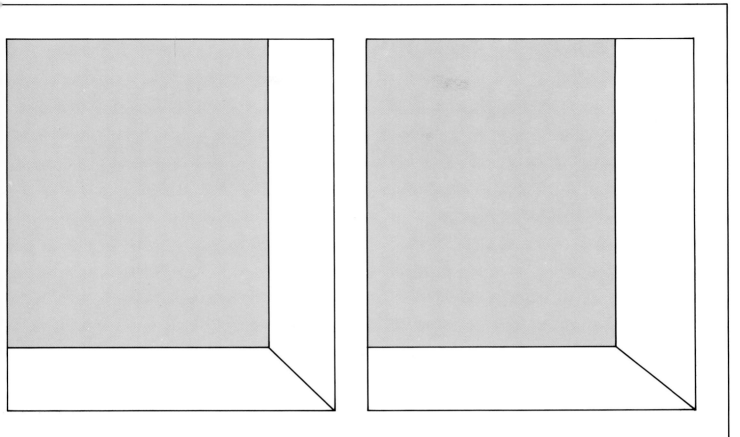

*Appendix:*

# DESIGNERS AND SOURCES OF SUPPLY

# Sources

The following mail order companies distribute closet organizing systems and accessories:

**Boston Proper Mail Order**
1 Boston Plaza
P.O. Box 1457
Mount Vernon, NY 10551
(800) 243-4300

**Conran's Mail Order**
Dept. 9039
1690 Oak Street
P.O. Box 1412
Lakewood, NJ 08707
(201) 905-8800
15 stores throughout the East Coast

**Hold Everything**
Williams-Sonoma
Mail Order Department
P.O. Box 7456
San Francisco, CA 94120
(415) 652-9007

**Joan Cook**
P.O. Box 21628
Ft. Lauderdale, FL 33335
(800) 327-3799

**Lillian Vernon**
510 South Fulton Avenue
Mount Vernon, NY 10550
(914) 633-6300

**Solutions**
P.O. Box 6878
Portland, OR 97228
(800) 342-9988

**Tapestry**
Hanover House Industries
Catalog Request
340 Popular Street
Hanover, PA 17331
(800) 621-5800

The following companies manufacture and/or distribute closet organizing systems and accessories:

## NATIONAL

**California Closets**
6409 Independence Avenue
Woodland Hills, CA 91367
(800) 345-6333
75 stores nationwide

## CALIFORNIA

**Maxine Ordesky**
240 South Linden Drive
Beverly Hills, CA 90212
(213) 277-0499

**K-C Products Company, Inc.**
1600 East Sixth Street
Los Angeles, CA 90023
(213) 267-1600

**Salutations Ltd.**
11640 San Vincente Boulevard
Los Angeles, CA 90049
(213) 820-6127

**Space Options**
1820 Westwood Boulevard
Los Angeles, CA 90025
(213) 470-4207

**Hold Everything**
Village at Corte Madera
1520 Redwood Highway
Corte Madera, CA 94925
(415) 924-9550

Southcoast Plaza #2
3333 Bear Street #302
Costa Mesa, CA 92626
(714) 540-7155

Century City Shopping Center
#470
10250 Santa Monica Blvd.
Los Angeles, CA 90067
(213) 556-2188

## COLORADO

**Enderby**
2045 South Valentia Street
Suite 1
Denver, CO 80231
(303) 337-4402

## FLORIDA

**Closet Maid**
**Clairson International**
720 Southwest 17th Street
Ocala, FL 32674
(904) 732-8734

## ILLINOIS

**Space Options**
2506 North Clark Street
Chicago, IL 60614
(312) 528-7200

## MASSACHUSETTS

**Bath and Closet Boutique, Inc.**
139-A Newbury Street
Boston, MA 02116
(617) 267-6564

**Placewares**
351 Congress Street
Boston, MA 02210
(617) 451-2074

## MICHIGAN

**Clutter Control, Inc.**
28956 Orchard Lake Road
Farmington Hills, MI 48018
(313) 855-9678

## MINNESOTA

**Designworks**
2817 Hennepin Avenue
Minneapolis, MN 55408
(612) 872-0330

## NEW JERSEY

**Basic Line, Inc.**
17 Industrial Drive
Cliffwood Beach, NJ 07735
(201) 583-5820

**Corr-Pak International**
19 Kimberly Road
East Brunswick, NJ 08816
(201) 390-9600

**Elfa**
P.O. Box 3346
Princeton, NJ 08540
(609) 683-0660

## NEW YORK

**Closet King**
880 Lexington Avenue
New York, NY 10021
(212) 288-7871

**Closet Systems Corp.**
1175 Broadway
Hewlett, NY 11557
(516) 569-1400

**Conran's**
160 East 54th Street
New York, NY 10022
(212) 371-2225

**Creative Closets**
2408 Broadway
New York, NY 10024
(212)496-2473

**Eagle Associates**
101-01 Avenue D
Brooklyn, NY 11236
(718) 649-8007

**ICF (Interlubke)**
305 East 63rd Street
New York, NY 10021
(212) 750-0900

## PENNSYLVANIA

**Independent Products, Inc.**
420 Moyer Boulevard
West Point, PA 19486
(215) 699-2255

**Boston**
160 Newbury Street Boston MA 02116
(617) 267-5460

**Cambridge**
1378 Cambridge Street Cambridge MA 02139
(617) 491-8670

**Belmont Center**
59 Leonard Street Belmont Center MA 02178
(617) 489-3555

**Newton Centre**
796 Beacon Street Newton Centre MA 02159
(617) 527-9170

**Wellesley**
68 Central Street Wellesley MA 02181
(617) 237-2860

**Concord**
13 Walden Street Concord MA 01742
(508) 369-1590

**Burlington**
Burlington Mall Burlington MA 01803
(617) 270-7969

# Index